American Sign Language

for
dummies®
A Wiley Brand

T0355124

American Sign Language

Language

for **dummies**®

A Wiley Brand

by Adan R. Penilla II, PhD

Angela Lee Taylor

for **dummies**®

A Wiley Brand

American Sign Language For Dummies®

Published by: **John Wiley & Sons, Inc.**, 111 River Street, Hoboken, NJ 07030-5774, www.wiley.com

Copyright © 2017 by John Wiley & Sons, Inc., Hoboken, New Jersey

Published simultaneously in Canada

For general information on our other products and services, please contact our Customer Care Department within the U.S. at 877-762-2974, outside the U.S. at 317-572-3993, or fax 317-572-4002. For technical support, please visit https://hub.wiley.com/community/support/dummies.

Wiley publishes in a variety of print and electronic formats and by print-on-demand. Some material included with standard print versions of this book may not be included in e-books or in print-on-demand. If this book refers to media such as a CD or DVD that is not included in the version you purchased, you may download this material at http://booksupport.wiley.com. For more information about Wiley products, visit www.wiley.com.

Library of Congress Control Number: 2016953540

ISBN 978-1-119-28607-3 (pbk); ISBN 978-1-119-28609-7 (ebk); ISBN 978-1-119-28610-3 (ebk)

10 9 8 7 6 5 4 3 2 1

Contents at a Glance

Table of Contents

Introduction

American Sign Language is one of those fascinating forms of communication. As you walk through a grocery store, a restaurant, or a park, you might see some people moving their hands in the air as they look at each other. We know that they are communicating because they are responding to each other with gestures and facial expressions. There is meaning to the movement. How often have you thought that you would love to know how to do that? Well here is your chance.

About This Book

American Sign Language For Dummies is designed to give you a general understanding of how to communicate in American Sign Language, as well as a general understanding of Deaf culture and Deaf history. As you'll soon see, the language and the culture go hand in hand and can't be separated, and an understanding of both makes you a better signer. As you go through this book, you will see that ASL has rules about how to shape the hands, how the hands move, and how to put signs in order.

To clarify, this book focuses solely on what's known as *American Sign Language* (ASL) because it's pretty much the only form of communication for the Deaf community in the United States.

This book is categorized according to subject. You can use each chapter as a building block for the next chapter or you can skip around wherever you please. Just find a subject that interests you and dig in, remembering that the most important thing is to have fun while you're figuring out this stuff. It never hurts to have a study buddy. Having a friend to watch you sign, bounce off your questions, and applaud your progress may be just the thing. And if you like to fly solo, that's ok too. Whichever way you go, the construct of the book is simple enough to follow.

After you understand a concept, we strongly recommend that you practice with those who are already proficient. Conversing with Deaf people is highly recommended as they are the experts. Doing so helps reinforce the knowledge you obtain from this book and allows others to help you hone your skills. If others understand you, you're probably on the right track. And if you don't understand something, don't despair. People all over the world learn how to sign. You'll get there with practice.

Here are some conventions we use to help you navigate this book:

>> We capitalize the word *Sign* when we use it as another name for American Sign Language. We don't, however, capitalize it when we use it as a verb *(to sign)* or a noun (referring to a person — a *signer* — or to a specific sign).

>> We always capitalize *Deaf* because it means culturally Deaf (whereas lower-case "deaf" simply means that someone has an audiological hearing loss and communicates in spoken English rather than ASL).

>> Whenever we use Sign in lists, examples, and dialogues, we print it in ALL CAPS to show that it's the closest equivalent to its English counterpart.

>> When we introduce a new sign, we **bold** it in the text so that you know you're about to learn a new sign.

>> ASL doesn't use punctuation, so we add hyphens to show slight pauses in Sign translations.

>> The text (Sign and its English translation) always comes before the illustration.

>> To save space, manual numbers and words that are fingerspelled don't have illustrations. See Chapter 1 if you need help remembering how to sign a particular letter or number.

>> A **Q** in a line of ASL indicates that you need to sign the manual question mark (flip to Chapter 6 for more on the manual question mark).

Don't think of the translations of English sentences into ASL as word-for-word translations. In fact, many signs have no English equivalents. Throughout this book, you find English equivalents that are close in meaning to Sign but not exactly the same. Remember that ASL is a completely different language from English. Fortunately, many gestures that hearing people use are also used by Deaf people in ASL, so you already have a head start that you can build on.

Foolish Assumptions

We hate to assume anything about anyone, but when writing this book, we had to make a few foolish assumptions about you. Here they are (we hope we were right):

>> You have little or no experience in this type of communication, but you'll try anything once. Fair is fair.

>> You don't expect to become fluent in Sign after going through this book. You just want some basic vocabulary, and you want to see what particular signs look like by themselves and in simple sentences. There is nothing like intellectual curiosity.

>> You aren't interested in memorizing grammar rules; you just want to communicate. However, for you grammar gurus, Chapter 2 is written for you. There are rules and concepts sprinkled throughout the book.

>> You want to know a few signs to be able to communicate with Deaf friends, family members, and acquaintances. There is strength in thinking of others.

>> Because ASL satisfies a foreign language requirement at your college or university. Good for you!

>> You met an interesting Deaf girl or engaging Deaf guy, and knowing some Sign will really help out. At least you're honest.

Icons Used in This Book

To help you find certain types of information more easily, we include several icons in this book. You find them on the left-hand side of the page, sprinkled throughout:

TIP

This icon highlights tips and tricks that can make signing easier.

REMEMBER

This icon points out interesting and important information that you don't want to forget.

WARNING

To avoid making a blunder or offending a Deaf friend, pay attention to what these paragraphs have to say.

CULTURAL WISDOM

This icon draws your attention to information about the culture of the Deaf community.

PLAY THIS

This icon indicates "Signin' the Sign" dialogues and other elements that are featured in video clips online. You can see Sign in action and practice with the signers.

Beyond the Book

This book comes with an online Cheat Sheet that contains helpful reference information. To get the Cheat Sheet, go to www.dummies.com and type "American Sign Language For Dummies Cheat Sheet" in the Search box.

Your purchase of this book also gives you access to lots of online videos. Many of the dialogues in this book are shown online (as indicated by the Play This icon), and you'll also find a handy mini dictionary of common terms. You can access all of the videos at www.dummies.com/go/aslvideos.

Where to Go from Here

The beauty of this book is that you can begin anywhere you want. You may find it helpful to start with the first few chapters to get down the basics, but if that's not your thing, feel free to jump in wherever you want. Use the table of contents and the index to point you in the right direction (no pun intended). Find a subject that interests you, start signing, and have fun! Just remember, you're going to make mistakes, but don't let that discourage you. Instead, use those mistakes as opportunities to solidify and strengthen what you now know to be right. Nothing worthwhile comes easily.

1

American Sign Language and You

Trying out the signs you already know.

Structuring what you know and adding to your foundation.

Learning some basic expressions, numbers, and new vocabulary.

Building on your base of knowledge with things you know from home.

Chapter 1

You Already Know a Little Sign

Signing isn't difficult, although moving your hands, body, and face to convey meaning instead of just using your voice may seem odd at first. But with time, practice, and interaction, you'll see that hand movements can be meaningful. Your goal and reward is being able to meet and communicate with a whole new group of people — people who share your opinions, hobbies, and more. That's definitely worth the initial awkwardness!

This chapter illustrates the manual alphabet in American Sign Language and talks about hand and body movements. Here, we show you the basics of making handshapes and using facial expressions and body language to get your ideas across. And we start off by reassuring you that you already know some signs. Trust us — you do.

For example, Sign is interwoven in your gestures when you use your index finger to motion to someone to "come here," when you shake your head "yes" and "no," and when you give someone the "evil eye." When you put these in signing context, you convey volumes of information.

Discovering Signs That Look like What They Mean

Iconic or *natural* signs look like what they mean — the up and down motion of brushing your teeth that means **toothbrush,** for instance, or the right and left punches that mean **boxing.** Iconic signs always show action. Here are some examples:

BOXING: Looks like you're "putting up your dukes."

DRIVE: Pretend that you're steering a car.

EAT: Act like you're putting food in your mouth.

MILK: Have you ever seen a cow being milked? That's how you sign milk.

SWIMMING/POOL: Think of when you walk through the shallow end of the pool and extend your arms out in front of you to clear the water.

TOOTHBRUSH/BRUSH TEETH: If you've ever brushed your teeth with your finger, you made the sign for toothbrush and for brushing your teeth.

BEING A WINNING RECEIVER

If you have trouble reading someone's signs, check the context and then ask yourself, "What could this person mean?" Remember that it's okay to ask someone to repeat something, just like you do when you don't understand someone speaking to you. You can show a signer you're "listening" by nodding your head. If at any time someone is signing something to you and you begin not to understand, stop the person and let her know what you did understand and where you stopped understanding. This is perfectly acceptable. Don't wait for the person to finish a long, drawn-out thought and then say, "I don't understand."

Remember not to watch the signer's hands primarily. You want to watch the signer's hands through your peripheral vision. Keep your eyes on the whole picture, from the signer's abdomen on up to her head. The eyes, face, hands, and body movements tell the whole story.

Like the sign for boxing, many sports signs are iconic. Check out Chapter 12 for more sports signs.

Building on the Basics of Sign: Gestures and Expression

You already know that "speaking" ASL is mostly a matter of using your fingers, hands, and arms. What you may not understand yet is that facial expressions and body language are important and sometimes crucial for conveying and understanding signs and their meaning. If you're focused only on a signer's hands, you can easily miss the slightest rolling of the eyes, a raised eyebrow, or the signer "pointing" at something with the eyes. So expect to see hands on hips in frustration, eyes open wide in shock, and hands on mouths covering a hearty laugh. You know these gestures already and are off to a good start.

The following sections explain how you get nearly your whole body involved in ASL.

Spelling with your fingers

Signers use the manual alphabet (shown later in this section) all the time, especially beginners. Signers *fingerspell* — spell using the manual alphabet — certain words and, at first, people's names. So as a beginner, feel free to fingerspell any word you don't know the sign for. If you want to fingerspell two or more words in a row, such as a title or someone's first and last name, pause for just a second between each word.

REMEMBER

In this book, any word that you fingerspell is shown in hyphenated letters. For example, *mall* is written as M-A-L-L. We usually don't take the space to show the hand signs for each letter; we leave it to you to find the appropriate letters here in this chapter.

TIP

Don't worry about being slow at fingerspelling. Remember, clarity is the goal, not speed. Silently mouth the letter sounds as you fingerspell the letters. Doing so helps you control your speed because you concentrate more on the letters. Don't pronounce each letter individually; pronounce the sounds as you fingerspell. If you're fingerspelling P-H-I-L-L-I-P, for example, mouthing "P-H" is incorrect. You want to mouth the "F" sound.

You may encounter Deaf people who fingerspell everything, even words that have a sign. This is called the *Rochester Method,* and some Deaf people are most comfortable communicating this way. Even the best interpreters can easily get lost trying to understand this method. The best way to follow what these signers are expressing is to watch their mouth movement and read their lips. You may not catch most of what's said, but if you do some lip-reading, remember the topic, and ask for clarification, you'll get by.

PLAY THIS

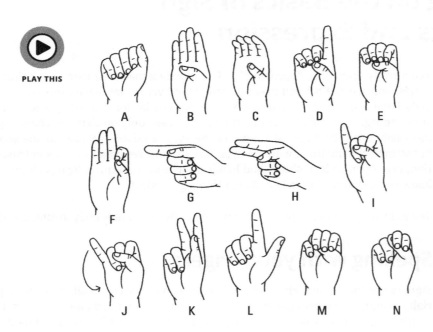

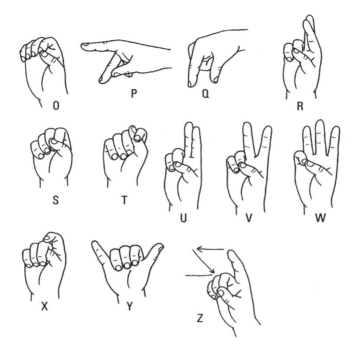

You sign, rather than fingerspell, some *initializations* — concepts such as **a.m.** and **p.m.**, which you sign as morning and evening, respectively. But you can finger-spell a word like **okay** as O-K, or you can just show the F handshape. Yes, it's a gesture, but it gets the point across. Remember, all languages use gestures, and ASL is no different.

TIP

A.M.

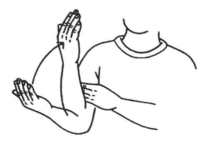

P.M.

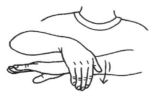

You may run across compound names that are abbreviated as two letters: Los Angeles (LA), San Francisco (SF), Burger King (BK), and Blue Ridge (BR). Remember to fingerspell the complete word before you abbreviate it, because L–A could mean Louisiana and B–R could mean Baton Rouge. The goal is to be clear; shortcuts and slang will come, so don't get ahead of yourself.

Shaping up those hands

Remembering a few simple points can help you make handshapes like a lifelong signer. *Handshapes* are hand formations that you use to sign each letter of the alphabet; this is also called the *manual alphabet.* Your manual dexterity is like a voice that has the ability to sing, and it requires practice. Start with two-letter words and graduate to larger ones. As you start getting the feel for fingerspelling, you'll be using hand muscles that you didn't know you had, so you may notice a little soreness.

REMEMBER

Handshapes are the individual letters of the manual alphabet, and fingerspelling is an action using the manual alphabet to create words.

WARNING

In your excitement to sign, you face the possibility of overusing your hands. Like that singing voice, your hands need a little break as they get ready for the next step. To find out how to keep your hands limber, search for "hand exercises" on the Internet or talk to sign language interpreters.

In the rest of this section, we explain the basic conventions of handshapes.

REMEMBER

For signing purposes, the hand you write with is called your *dominant hand* (some folks call it the *active hand*). The other hand is your *base hand* or *passive hand.* In this book, all the illustrations represent a right-handed signer — the right hand illustrates the dominant hand, and the left hand illustrates the passive hand. So, in a nutshell, if you see a sign with the right hand dominant and you're left-handed, use your left hand.

While your active hand does the work, your passive hand does one of the following:

>> It mirrors the active hand.

>> It displays one of seven basic handshapes, called *natural handshapes.*

The seven natural handshapes are the letters **A, B, C, S,** and **O** and the numbers **1** and **5.**

If you don't use your passive hand for these handshapes, you'll be breaking a rule in ASL. The Deaf person who is watching you sign may not know this particular rule, but they'll be thrown off. Therefore, follow this basic rule and stay ahead of the game.

You can use natural handshapes in a variety of ways. You may form the same handshape in one direction for a particular sign but in a different direction for another sign. For a sign such as **start,** you form the natural handshape (in this case, the number 5) in one direction. But for a sign such as **cook,** you form that same natural handshape in a different direction. Check out the following examples of active/passive handshapes that you use while signing:

START: Place your active index finger between your index and middle fingers of your passive hand, and then turn the active index finger outward — it looks like you're turning the ignition key in a car.

BUY: Hold out your passive hand, palm up in the 5 handshape. Use your active hand as you would to hand money to a salesclerk.

COOK: Hold your passive hand out, palm up. Lay your active hand across the top of it, palm down. Now flip your active hand over, then flip it back over, palm down.

When your passive hand mirrors the shape of your dominant hand, you move both hands either together or alternately. If moving them alternately, you move both hands in alternate directions at the same time. Here are some examples of alternating handshapes:

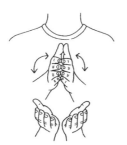

BOOK: Make this sign as if you're actually opening a book.

GIFT: Put both hands in front of you in the "X" handshape, but extend one a little farther away than the other from your body. At the same time, jerk your hands up a little bit, twice.

MAYBE: With both hands facing upward, alternate them in an up down motion.

STORE: Keep your hands in the same shape and move them back and forth simultaneously.

Benefiting with body language

Communicating a concept in Sign is often made clear by using body language. The meaning of **I don't know** comes through clearly when you raise your shoulders, tilt your head, and turn your palm up. Signing **I'm sick** is more easily understood when you accompany the sign with half-shut eyes, an open mouth, and a partially extended tongue. Another example is the word **no.** The speed at which you shake your head from side to side, with eyes open or shut, can say a lot about the degree of **no.** Quick, short body movements show an emphatic message; an exaggeratedly slow motion with an exaggerated facial expression conveys a similar message. In a word, the speed of the sign displays various tones. Check out the illustrations of these signs to see what we mean:

DON'T KNOW: This Sign should convey an actual look of not knowing. It makes the Sign more authentic.

SICK: Both hands move in a small circular motion. One hand touches the head while the other touches the stomach. Looking nauseous as you do the sign. The facial expression is the ticket to signing this term correctly.

NO: When you sign the word, close your eyes if you want to make it more emphatic. This sign can be made as gentle as telling your favorite niece, *no,* or as harshly as possible by telling a pest, *NO!* Attitude is everything in ASL.

Gazing at the face of expression

In Sign, you use your face to show emotion and add expression. Facial expressions tell you how the signer feels about the information he's signing. Your facial expression is just as important as your hand movements. Without the correct facial expression, the person watching you sign will either get the wrong message or need clarification to make sure that he understands your message correctly.

Don't be alarmed if you aren't understood, even if a Deaf person asks for clarification a couple of times for the same sentence. This means the person genuinely wants to understand what you mean, and it also affords you the opportunity to learn to express your thoughts by Deaf standards. This is an invaluable way of learning; don't shy away from this experience.

Sign expressions as if you actually "feel" that way. For example, you sign the word **sad** while you slump your shoulders down and make a sad facial expression. You sign **happy** just the opposite — keep your shoulders up and wear a smile. (Check out Chapter 3 for illustrations of these signs.)

REMEMBER

Be sure that you maintain eye contact when you're signing, and, again, watch your conversational partner's face, not his hands. Your peripheral vision allows you to still see the hands, so don't worry about missing any signs.

Signin' the Sign

Belinda and Terry are getting ready for the holidays. Belinda wants to start shopping for Christmas presents.

Terry: Do you want a ride to the mall?
Sign: M-A-L-L — RIDE — WANT YOU Q

 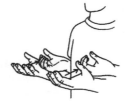 

Belinda: Yes, I want to start buying Christmas gifts soon.
Sign: YES — SOON — CHRISTMAS GIFTS — START BUYING — WANT ME

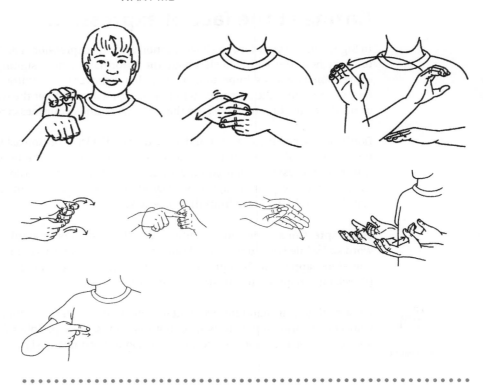

Chapter 2

Signing Grammar Basics

I n this chapter, we talk about the building blocks that you need to communicate in any language — nouns, verbs, adjectives, and adverbs — and we tell you how to put them together to form simple sentences. We also tell you how to get your body involved to express verb tenses.

Explaining the Parts of Speech

Both English and American Sign Language have subjects and verbs, as well as adjectives and adverbs that describe the subjects and verbs. Also, English and Sign both allow you to converse about the present, past, and future, so whatever English can do, Sign can do — visually. However, unlike English, ASL doesn't use prepositions as a separate part of speech. As a general rule, most prepositions in Sign, with a few exceptions, act as verbs.

REMEMBER

The English language articles — *a, an,* and *the* — aren't used in Sign. Likewise, helping verbs, such as *am, is,* and *are,* aren't used in Sign, either. ASL is an active language, which means that helping verbs and being verbs aren't necessary.

Distinguishing between noun/verb pairs

Some nouns and verbs in Sign share the same handshapes. You distinguish the part of speech by signing the motion once if it's a verb and twice if it's a noun. Like any language, there are exceptions to the rule.

Though most nouns don't have a verb that looks the same, all but a few nouns need the double motion. Most of the noun illustrations in this book are represented by double arrows. We indicate which nouns don't follow the double-motion rule.

Table 2-1 shows a few noun and verb pairs.

TABLE 2-1 **Nouns and Verbs with Shared Handshapes**

English Noun	Sign	English Verb	Sign
CHAIR		SIT	
PLANE		FLY	
CAR		DRIVE	

The following examples compare the noun/verb differences.

English: Please sit in this chair.
Sign: THIS CHAIR (point) — PLEASE — SIT

English: I like to fly small planes.
Sign: SMALL PLANES — FLY — LIKE ME

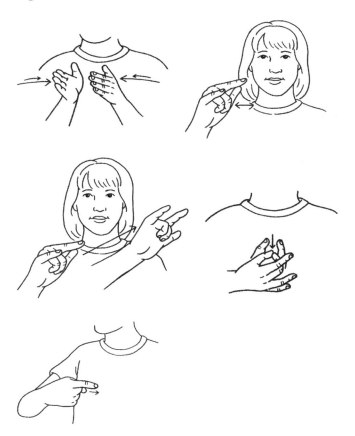

Modifying with adjectives and adverbs

In English, a modifier can come before or after the word it modifies, depending on the sentence. However, in Sign, you typically place the adjective or adverb — the modifier — after the word it modifies. But sometimes in Sign, you may find yourself expressing the modifier at the same time you sign the word it modifies, just by using your face.

Your facial expressions can describe things and actions in ASL. For instance, if something is small or big, you can show its size without actually signing **small** or **big.** You can describe a small piece of thread by pursing your lips, blowing out a little air, and closing your eyes halfway. If something is very thick, puff out your cheeks. You can convey that it's raining hard or that a car is moving fast by moving your eyebrows or shaping your mouth a certain way. (Turn to Chapter 1 for more on using expressions and body language.)

The following examples show adjectives and adverbs placed with nouns and verbs. We also provide tips on how to use facial expressions to really get your point across when describing things in Sign.

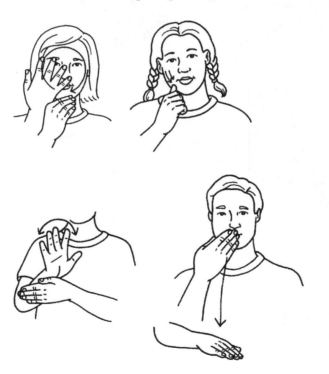

PRETTY GIRL: Raise your eyebrows, form your mouth into an "o" shape (like saying ooh), sign "pretty" and then "girl."

BAD MOVIE: Sign the word "movie" and then turn your mouth down in a frown and scrunch your eyebrows together while signing the word "bad."

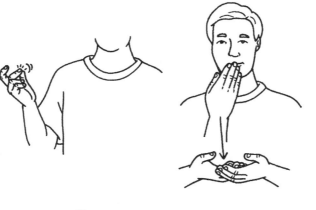

GOOD DOG:
Sign the word "dog" first, then slightly smile and raise your eyebrows as you sign the word "good."

TALK LOUDLY or LOUDLY TALK

RUN VERY FAST:
Sign the word "run" while scrunching your eyebrows together and clenching your jaw tight with your mouth slightly open.

REMEMBER

Some adverbs used in English, such as the words *very* and *really*, are also used in ASL. Others must be incorporated into the verb by using facial expressions.

Talking Tenses

To communicate tenses in Sign, you need your hands *and* your body. Showing tense in ASL is partly a matter of where you sign in relation to your body.

Think of your body as being in the present tense, which is a fairly safe assumption, we hope.

To place everything you sign into past tense, you sign **finish** at chest level or higher, depending on the level of intensity, at either the beginning or end of the sentence (most signers do it at the beginning for clarity), while saying the word *fish*, a shortened version of *finish.* This sign signals that everything has already happened.

You can also use the **finish** sign when making an exclamation. (For more on this sign's uses, see the section "Exclaiming in Simple Sentences" later in this chapter.)

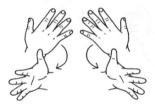

Signing in future tense works pretty much the same way as signing in past tense. You indicate future tense by signing and saying **will** at the end of a sentence. The farther you sign the word **will** from the front of your body, the farther into the future you go. Here's an example:

English: He will go later.
Sign: HE GO — WILL

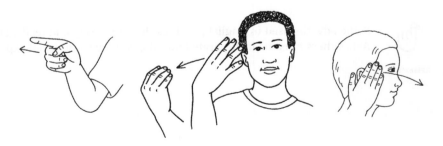

You can also sign **will** to show affirmation. For example:

English: Mike is walking over to my house.
Sign: MY HOUSE — M-I-K-E — WALK— WILL

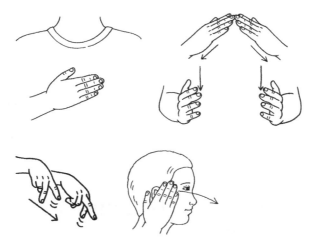

You can easily sign an event that's going to happen in the future. A simple rule to follow: Mention what's planned or intended and then sign **will.**

REMEMBER

Here's a time-sensitive concept that doesn't quite fit into past, present, or future tense. To show that you're not yet finished with or you haven't even started a task, sign the unaccomplished deed and then sign **not yet** while shaking your head slightly from side to side, as if saying *no,* at the end of the sentence. You don't pronounce *not yet,* though; you simply sign it. The following sentence gives you an idea of how you can use this expression:

English: I haven't eaten.
Sign: ME EAT — NOT YET

Structuring Sentences

Putting a sentence together in English is pretty basic. You usually put it in subject-verb-direct object order, perhaps throwing in an indirect object between the verb and the direct object. In ASL, however, you can choose to assemble your sentence in different orders, depending on the dialogue.

You can sign simple sentences in a natural English order. However, most of the time, you can get your point across in a variety of ways.

Although Sign is an official language, it isn't a written one. Some people have attempted to make an artificial Sign system for writing purposes, but few people know it because its use is so limited. Because ASL isn't meant to be a written language, it has no punctuation. To write about Sign, as in this book, you must translate it as closely as possible into a written language such as English.

Subjecting yourself to nouns and verbs in simple sentences

Unlike English grammar rules, which dictate that the subject must go before the verb, Sign allows you to put the subject before or after the verb when dealing with simple sentences; it doesn't matter which word comes first. The same goes for exclamations; you can place them at the beginning or the end of a simple sentence (see the section "Exclaiming in Simple Sentences" later in this chapter). The following examples illustrate how simple sentences work.

English: He ran.
Sign: HE RAN
Sign: RAN HIM

English: She fell.
Sign: SHE FELL
Sign: FELL HER

Placing subjects and objects

To incorporate direct and indirect objects into your signing, first start with a basic subject-verb sentence. You can sign it in subject-verb or verb-subject order. Here are some examples:

English: He sells.
Sign: HE SELLS

English: I eat.
Sign: ME EAT

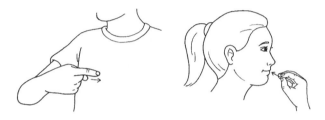

English: She drives.
Sign: SHE DRIVES

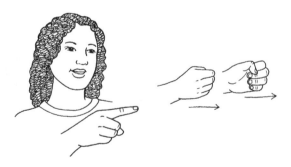

Although these short sentences get the point across, the world would be pretty boring if that's how people communicated all the time. So add a direct object to each of these sentences to make them a little more interesting.

In case you haven't had a grammar class in a few years, a *direct object* is a word that goes after the verb and answers the question *what?* or *whom?* However, in ASL, the direct object can go either before the subject or after the verb.

English: He sells food.
Sign: HE SELLS FOOD

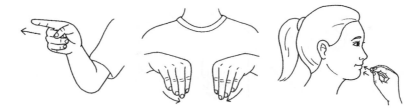

Sign: FOOD HE SELLS

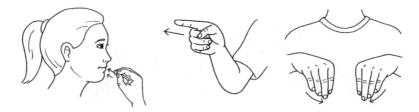

English: I eat pizza.
Sign: ME EAT PIZZA

Sign: PIZZA ME EAT

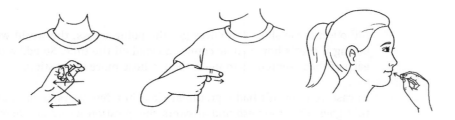

English: She drives a car.
Sign: SHE DRIVES CAR

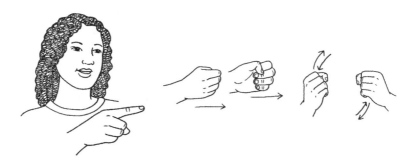

Sign: CAR SHE DRIVES

If you have a sentence that may be misunderstood if you change the word order, leave it in the natural English order. For example, if you want to say *Joe loves Sue*, you need to sign JOE LOVES SUE. Changing it around to SUE LOVES JOE doesn't convey the same meaning. (Having said that, we really hope that Sue does love Joe in return.)

Okay. So you're signing sentences with direct objects. Now, try to take your signing skills one step further by signing *indirect objects*. (Another quick grammar reminder: Indirect objects are words that come between the verb and direct object; they indicate who or what receives the direct object.) You place the indirect object right after the subject and then show the action. These sentences show you the correct order:

English: The girl throws the dog a bone.
Sign: DOG BONE — GIRL — THROW

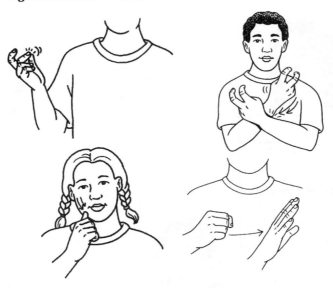

English: I gave the teacher an apple.
Sign: ME TEACHER — APPLE GAVE

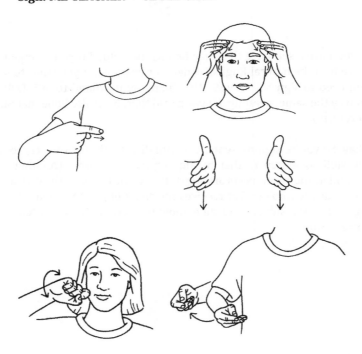

CULTURAL WISDOM

Signing sentences in an understandable order may be a bit tricky at first. If the person you're signing to is leaning forward, has an inquisitive look, or seems distracted, he or she probably doesn't understand you. You may want to try signing the thought in a different way.

Signin' the Sign

Linda and Buddy are at work. The restaurant will be opening in one hour, and they're taking a quick breather before it opens.

Linda: The chairs look nice.
Sign: CHAIRS — LOOK NICE

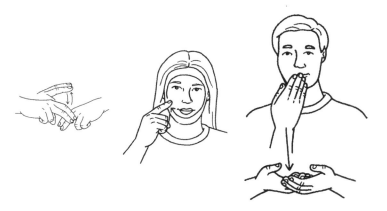

Buddy: That pizza smells good.
Sign: PIZZA — SMELLS GOOD

Linda: We're finished. I'm going to eat now.
Sign: WE FINISH — NOW — ME EAT

  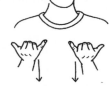

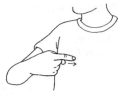 

Buddy: Sit. I'll bring you some pizza.
Sign: SIT — PIZZA — BRING YOU — WILL

Linda:	Throw me an apple, too.
Sign:	APPLE — THROW ME — TOO

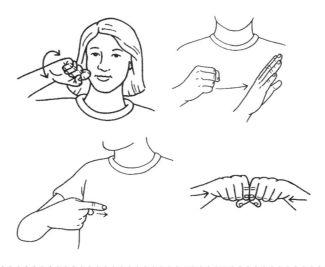

Exclaiming in Simple Sentences

Exclamations in all languages tell the listener how you feel about a subject. Sign is no different. Exclamation is used a lot in Sign; both signer and receiver use it. As in English, you can also use exclamation to show *how* strong you feel or don't feel about something. Other signers who are watching can sign what they feel about what you've signed, too. You can sign exclamations at the beginning or end of the sentence. Most, but not all, exclamations in Sign have English equivalents. Following is a list of some of the more popular Sign exclamations. Ask your Deaf friends to sign these expressions to get a clear picture because the face will tell a thousand words.

OH/I SEE

WHAT: This exclamation is fingerspelled simply as W-T; it's only used as a one-word exclamation (as "What?!").

FINISH: Although finish is used at the beginning of a sentence to show past tense (see the section "Talking Tenses" earlier in this chapter), it's also used as humor in Sign to indicate "enough already" and as a reprimand meaning "stop that." You sign the word, using just one hand, and you pronounce the word "fish," which is a shortened version of the sign for "finish," as stated earlier. You can tell by the context of the conversation which way it's being used.

OH MY GOSH

WOW

OOH: (Also known as "flick"): Start with your hand in the "8" handshape, then change it to a "5" sign handshape using a quick flicking motion with your middle finger.

COOL

Signin' the Sign

Adan and Aurora will be celebrating their 50th wedding anniversary. Adan wants to stay home and celebrate, while Aurora wants to go out. See how their conversation unfolds.

Aurora: Wow! Our 50th anniversary!
Sig.n: ANNIVERSARY — 50 YEARS — US — WOW

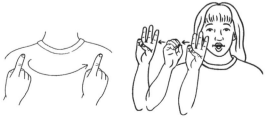

Adan: Ooh, that's a long time!
Sign: (flick!) — LONG TIME — SO FAR

Aurora: Where do you want to celebrate?
Sign: CELEBRATION — WHERE GO — Q

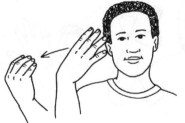 

Adan: The living room.
Sign: (point) — LIVING ROOM

Aurora: Oh, I see. Why?
Sign: OH I SEE WHY — Q

Adan: It's inexpensive.
Sign: CHEAP

Aurora: You stop that!
Sign: FINISH

· ·

Signing Conditional Sentences

A conditional sentence occurs when a circumstance is added to a sentence. A *circumstance* is a phrase that usually starts with a conditional word, such as "if" or "suppose."

TIP

Sign the conditional word while raising your eyebrows, but then follow with the rest of the conditional phrase and sentence with your eyebrows back down in their normal position.

Consider this example:

English: If you order beer, I'll order wine.
Sign: IF BEER ORDER YOU — WINE ORDER ME

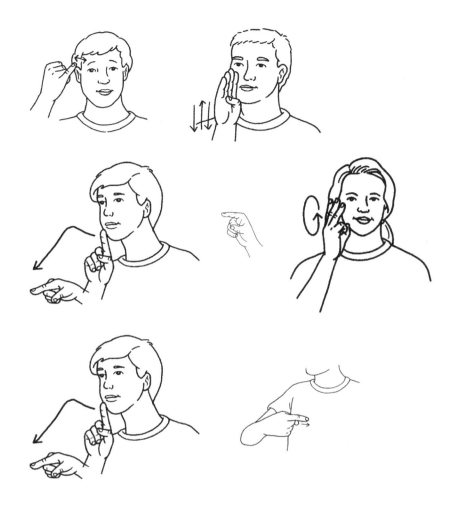

Personification: The Secret of Agents

In ASL, turning a verb into a person is called *personification.* You do it with two simple motions: Sign the verb and then glide the heels of your hands down the sides of your body with your fingers extended outward. The result of this is an **agent.** Look at this list to see what we mean.

WRITE + AGENT = WRITER

FLY + AGENT = PILOT

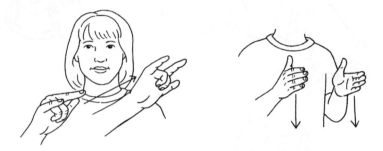

SUPERVISE + AGENT = SUPERVISOR

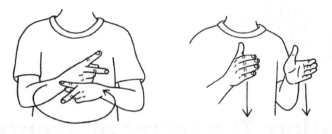

COOK + AGENT = CHEF

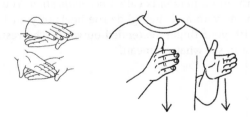

LAW + AGENT = LAWYER

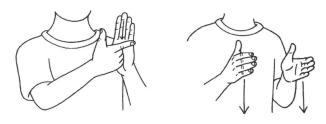

MANAGE + AGENT = MANAGER

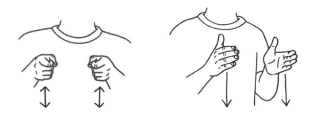

Clarifying with Classifiers

Classifiers in ASL may sound complicated but they are not; they are a fun way to explain the finer points of the message you are conveying. Once you get the hang of them, you can show off your skill to your Deaf friends and let them teach you more about classifiers.

Classifiers are nothing more than handshapes that are grouped into categories with a specific purpose as describing something, showing relationships, demonstrating something, or taking the place of an object. Therefore, think of them as handshapes that can represent a person, place, or a thing by showing how things are positioned or shaped. You can show what happens to these agents once they are set up as classifiers; classifiers clarify your point. This is why they are called *Size and Shape Classifiers*. Since classifiers show detailed information, do not use them until **after** you have explained the subject of the matter then explain the specifics by using classifiers. Classifiers will give the addressee all the specifics your hands can handle.

Here are some ideas to get you started. If you need a little help, let me give you a hand; go to the "Spelling with your fingers" section of Chapter 1 and see the handshapes for A, C, and F.

» **The manual letter-*A* handshape** with the thumb pointing upward can be any object that is erect as a vase, a stop sign on a street, or a computer tower on the floor. Identify the object first and then use the classifier to represent it.

» **The manual letter-*C* handshape** can be a muscle on an arm, a drinking glass, or a wad of dollars in the hand. This classifier can be anything in an arch shape.

» **The manual letter-*F* handshape** can be coins on a hand, small rocks, or polka dots on a shirt, anything in a small round shape.

Chapter 3

Starting to Sign Basic Expressions

This chapter sets you off on the right foot (or hand!) to meet and greet fellow signers and start signing basic expressions. You can acquaint yourself with American Sign Language by watching Deaf people sign. Being included in a conversation is a great transition for conversing in ASL. Don't worry about signing perfectly. Deaf people will know that you're a novice signer — just have fun with it.

REMEMBER

Interacting with other signers is an important part of getting the basics under your belt. You'll find that all signers, Deaf and hearing, have different styles. Like English, the words are the same, but no two people talk alike. Setting a goal to be clear is a must. Your style will come naturally.

Initiating a Conversation

Most people who learn ASL look forward to signing with others. Attending functions with other signers gives ample opportunity to practice Sign. At Deaf functions, signed conversation happens everywhere. If you're invited by a Deaf person, allow the person to introduce you to others — great conversations start this way. If you're on your own and want to strike up a conversation, this section tells you how to properly get someone's attention and provides some ideas for conversation starters.

REMEMBER

If Deaf people correct your signing, view this as a compliment and take no offense. They see you as a worthy investment.

WARNING

When you initiate a conversation, you want to avoid *to be* verbs. These verb types set up ASL conversation in the passive form of speaking, and ASL must always be in the active form. So if you use *to be* verbs, Deaf people will have difficulty reading your ASL. In a nutshell, follow this rule: Never sign *am, are, was, were, be, being,* or *been.* They aren't used in ASL. You may see signs for these words as you're out and about, but they've been invented to teach Deaf children English, so don't use them.

REMEMBER

Is, as a verb, does not have a hand in ASL. It is used for affirmation so put the Sign TRUE at the end of a sentence for anything declarative.

Attracting someone's attention

Attracting someone's attention is easy in English. A simple yell turns many heads. To get a Deaf person's attention, tap the person on the shoulder or the back of the arm between the elbow and the shoulder. Waving at someone is another good way to get attention. A wooden floor is also a big help — stomping on the floor is an acceptable and popular attention-getter. Deaf people feel the vibration on the floor and turn to see its origination.

REMEMBER

Another way to get someone's attention is to make and maintain eye contact. You can tell someone across a crowded room that you have something on your mind by catching the person's eye. And then, after eye contact has been made and you've approached each other, you can proceed with a conversation. Non-signers may view this action as staring and think that it's rude, but in the Deaf world, making and maintaining eye contact is a necessary common practice.

WARNING

Never throw objects at a Deaf person to get the person's attention. Besides being just plain rude, it's also dangerous. ASL is a visual language, so Deaf people really value their eyesight. Accidentally hitting someone in the eye could be devastating, and you could get hit back!

Using greetings and closings

Asking questions is probably the most popular way to start a conversation. You can ask a person's name, sign yours, ask what school the person attended, and so on. Many Deaf people attended one of the residential schools for the Deaf that are located throughout the United States; you may have a city in common. You can also start a conversation with a simple **hi** or **hello,** followed by **nice to meet you.** These greetings work with Deaf people of all ages. Signing **What's up?** is a simple, informal greeting that's a great opener, too.

Shaking hands and giving hugs are also common additions to Deaf greetings. Hand-shaking is more formal than hugging, just as is true in the hearing world.

You can join a conversation easily by using one of the following openings:

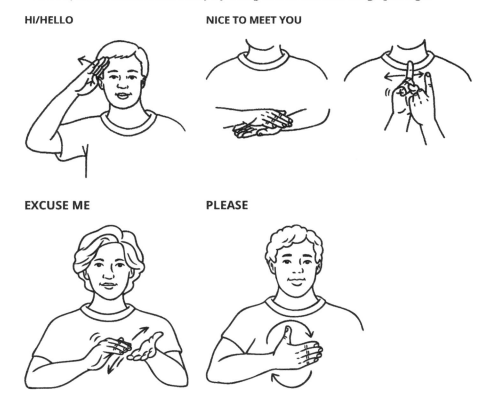

HI/HELLO

NICE TO MEET YOU

EXCUSE ME

PLEASE

HONORARY INTRO

HOW ARE YOU?

REMEMBER

If you ask a question, raise your eyebrows and tilt your head forward; doing so shows others that your sentence is a question and that you're waiting for a response. Try these simple questions:

English: Do you sign?
Sign: SIGN YOU Q

English: Are you deaf?
Sign: DEAF YOU Q

English: How are you?
Sign: WHAT'S UP

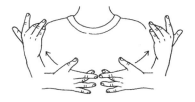

When you see two people standing close together and signing small, don't stare. They may be having a private conversation.

Chewing gum is a no-no in Sign. Mouth movement is an important part of signed communication. Do everyone a favor and keep chewing and signing separate.

When you're ready to end a conversation, here are a couple signs that are sure to help:

GOODBYE

SEE YOU LATER

YOU'RE WELCOME

Signin' the Sign

 Buddy and Della are at the park. Buddy sees Della make a gesture that looks like a sign and decides to approach her.

Buddy: Do you sign?
Sign: SIGN YOU Q

Della: Yes, are you deaf?
Sign: YES — DEAF YOU Q

Buddy: No, my sister is deaf.
Sign: NO — MY SISTER — DEAF

Della:	Oh, I see; you sign well.
Sign:	OH I SEE — SIGN SKILL YOU

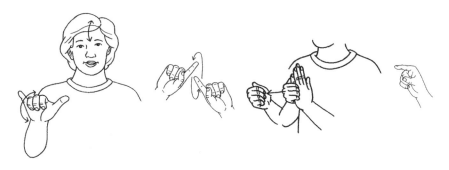

Getting Acquainted

Meeting new friends is always exciting. Getting acquainted with Deaf friends is very much like getting acquainted with people who hear, but you need to keep in mind a few important points. This section spells them out for you.

As you get acquainted with folks, keep these tips in mind:

» **During introductions, simply *fingerspell* (sign each letter individually) your name.** Deaf people are the only ones who give name signs. Those who can hear don't invent their own, nor do they give name signs to each other. (See the nearby sidebar for more on what exactly name signs are.)

Keep in mind that when someone asks you your name, sign your first and last name — it's good manners.

Titles, such as Mr., Mrs., and Ms., aren't used in ASL. Simply spell out the person's name.

» **Follow the conversation that's started and do your best to understand what you can.** If you don't catch something, don't interrupt the signer. Wait until they finished. You may be able to put it all together. It is possible that you will get the gist at the end of the conversation and won't need clarification.

» **Keep a steady hand.** Your signs are easier to read when your hand isn't shaking.

» **Ask questions for clarification.** Don't be embarrassed if you don't understand something. Asking questions is the best way to learn.

WHAT'S IN A NAME SIGN?

Name signs aren't formal names; they're manual letters that express some characteristic of a person, or even just a manual letter or letters that represent someone's name. Having a name sign allows everyone in the Deaf community to know who you're talking about and helps avoid constantly having to fingerspell someone's name. You sign name signs on the signer's body or in front of the signer. You normally make the handshape of the first letter of a person's first name and, sometimes, last name(s).

Signin' the Sign

Dee and Cameron are meeting for the first time. They're making their introductions.

Dee: Hi, I'm Dee.
Sign: HI — D-E-E ME

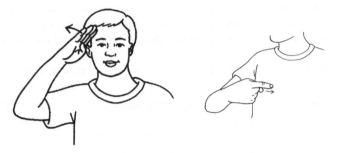

Cameron: Nice to meet you. I'm Cameron.
Sign: NICE MEET YOU — C-A-M-E-R-O-N ME

Dee: Nice to meet you, too.
Sign: NICE MEET TOO

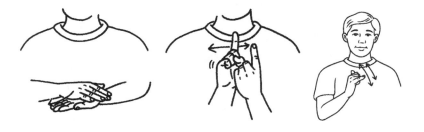

Sharing feelings and emotions

Sharing your feelings and emotions when signing is easy because Sign is naturally so expressive. Put your heart into what you're signing to genuinely express what you mean. You can express some feelings and emotions with minimal Sign and a lot of facial expressions because people already understand such expressions.

Take a look at some signs for feelings and emotions:

SAD

HAPPY

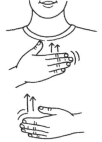

ANGRY

CURIOUS

Signin' the Sign

Dee and Buddy are at the store. Dee is shocked by the rising cost of everything. She shares her displeasure with Buddy.

Dee: Everything is so expensive!
Sign: EVERYTHING EXPENSIVE

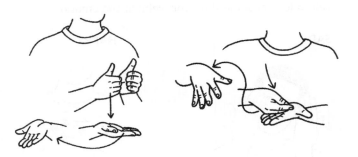

Buddy: Yes, and no sales.
Sign: TRUE — DISCOUNTS NONE

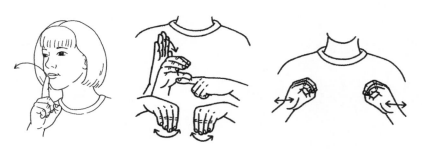

Dee: It's sad; even stamps are going up.
Sign: SAD — STAMP COST — INCREASE TOO

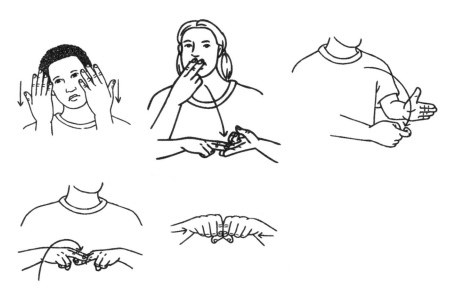

Buddy: It really makes me angry.
Sign: ANGRY ME

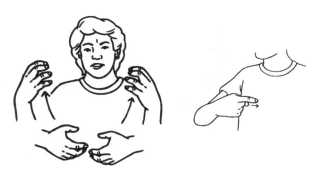

Dee: Me, too.
Sign: ME TOO

Connecting your thoughts

When you're ready to connect your thoughts in ASL, use the signs in this section for connectors. Remember that clarity is the key to a successful conversation, so as you add more information, look at the Deaf addressee and make sure that the person's facial expression is engaged. If the person asks you for clarification, don't shy away from your thoughts; the Deaf person is trying to follow along, so keep going!

ALSO

BUT

OR

OTHER

ADDITIONALLY

Talking about where you're from

Signing about where you're from is a great way to converse with a new friend. Because it can lead to other topics of conversation, it's a common icebreaker and will help you practice your Sign vocabulary. You can practice your fingerspelling — you may not know the sign of a particular location, or it may not have a sign — and expand your geographical knowledge. For example, you could sign about different famous landmarks and tourist sites.

Countries

REMEMBER

Signing in every country is different. Although some countries have similar sign languages, no two are exactly alike.

When two Deaf people from different countries meet, their chances of communicating are pretty good because they're both skilled at making their points known in their respective countries. Although their sign languages are different, their communication skills may involve mime, writing, gestures, and pointing. People who can hear can also do those things, but their communication skills are usually more dependent on listening to the spoken language.

WARNING

Some country name signs that are used in ASL are offensive to those respective countries. For instance, the ASL sign for Mexico also means "bandit," and the signs for Korea, Japan, and China are signed near the eye with a hand movement that indicates "slanted eyes." Many signers are now using the indigenous name signs that are politically correct and aren't offensive.

Here are the signs for the countries in North America:

CANADA

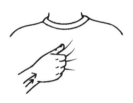

UNITED STATES/AMERICA

MEXICO

Here are the signs for some European countries:

ENGLAND

FRANCE

SPAIN

States, cities, and other locations

TIP

Many states and cities have name signs or abbreviations, but it's okay to ask someone to fingerspell a place if you don't understand.

Some common state and city signs are in Table 3-1.

TABLE 3-1   Signs for Various Cities and States

English	Sign	English	Sign
ARIZONA		ATLANTA	
CALIFORNIA		BOSTON	

(continued)

TABLE 3-1 *(continued)*

English	Sign	English	Sign
COLORADO		DENVER	
FLORIDA		HOUSTON	
KENTUCKY		LOS ANGELES	
MINNESOTA		MIAMI	
NEW YORK		PITTSBURGH	

English	Sign	English	Sign
TEXAS			

Signin' the Sign

 Lindsey is telling Angie about a road trip he and Buddy are taking to visit friends in several states.

Lindsey: Buddy and I are taking a trip.
Sign: B-U-D-D-Y (point) ME — TRAVEL — WILL

Angie: Wow! Sounds like a fun time.
Sign: WOW — SEEMS FUN

Lindsey: We're going to Texas, California, and Colorado.
Sign: US TRAVEL WHERE — TEXAS CALIFORNIA COLORADO

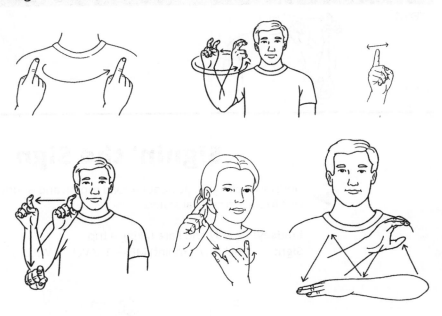

Angie: Will you see Chip?
Sign: YOU SEE C-H-I-P Q

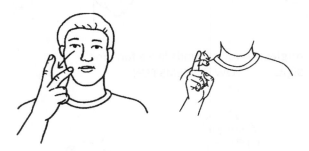

Lindsey: Yes, Chip's in Los Angeles.
Sign: YES — C-H-I-P LA

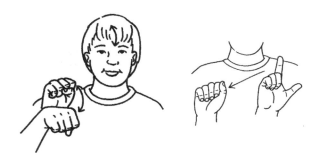

• •

Locations add the details to what you're signing. Details are the key to clear and precise conversation. The following location signs will help:

BRIDGE

LAKE

CORNER

TREE

MOUNTAIN

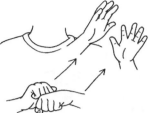

RIVER

FLOWER

GRASS

FOUNTAIN

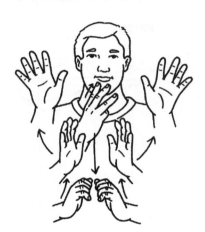

Signin' the Sign

Dee and Ted are in Japan. They're in awe of the beautiful country and are sharing their feelings about the experience.

Dee: The trees are beautiful in Japan.
Sign: JAPAN — TREES — BEAUTIFUL

Ted: The mountains are so high.
Sign: MOUNTAINS HIGH

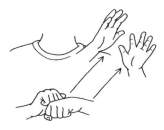

Dee: There are so many rivers.
Sign: RIVERS — MANY

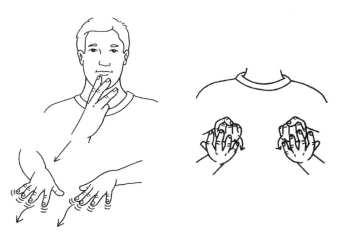

· ·

Acting the Part: Constructed Dialogue and Constructed Action

One thing people tend to do in English when they talk about a conversation is recall who said what to whom. Sometimes, the speaker has to clarify some things so the listener gets an accurate picture. In ASL, the picture is a lot clearer because you show, not tell. This type of communication has different names: *episodic signing, role shifting,* or *Constructed Action.* Constructed Action is the latest term because it has the latest research. Regardless of the term, the idea is to construct a picture for your addressee to convey what transpired in a conversation. Constructed Action describes the action of what occurred in a conversation, but there's also *Constructed Dialogue,* which focuses on what was said.

Constructed Dialogue

Constructed Dialogue is a way to communicate the details of what was said in a conversation. This technique requires your body to shift slightly from side to side so you can role shift. The purpose of this shift is to take on the character of the two people who had the conversation you're describing.

REMEMBER

When you engage in Constructed Dialogue, keep a couple of things in mind: Make sure the person with whom you're signing knows the names of the people you're talking about and also what the gist of the conversation between the two people was.

PLAY THIS

Here's a scenario to show you how Constructed Dialogue works: Sheri and Buddy are talking about Sheri's upcoming wedding. Sheri wants to let Buddy know that her aunts can't agree on the color of the cake. Sheri has already shared with Buddy what the problem is, who is involved, and their general thoughts on the subject.

Sheri shifts her body/waist to the left slightly and takes on the role of Aunt Dee, signing Aunt Dee's name once. After the shift, Sherri doesn't need to sign Aunt Dee's name again; she can just shift her body to the left. Aunt Dee, when referred to, remains in this position for the duration of the conversation.

Sheri signs: *Orange and cream are too Halloween-like; people are going to think it's a costume party.*

Because only two people are involved in the dialogue and Buddy knows who they are, introducing the name of the other participant, Aunt Denni, isn't necessary, but Sheri may sign Aunt Denni's name just to make sure she is clear.

Sheri shifts her body slightly to the right and begins to respond as if she is Aunt Denni: *Don't be silly, orange is Sheri's favorite color, and it is her big day after all.*

Sheri shifts to the left again, assuming Aunt Dee's position, and signs: *I think we need another opinion.*

Sheri shifts to the right again, taking on the role of Aunt Denni, and signs: *That really isn't necessary.*

After you understand the idea of Constructed Dialogue, start practicing it with others. You'll find that recalling the past with others isn't that difficult and that doing so adds a little complexity to your signing, allowing you to follow others with more certainty as they use Constructed Dialogue.

Constructed Action

Constructed Action is similar to Constructed Dialogue except that you sign actions instead of words from a conversation.

PLAY THIS

Here's a scenario: Wanda is talking to Della about the new dress she purchased to wear to a dinner last week. Wanda is telling Della that the dress fit fine at the mall, but on the night she wanted to wear it, the dress was too short!

Wanda shows Della exactly how she reacted by signing *put on the dress* and then *mirror*. Wanda looks into the mirror and signs *short* on her legs, exactly on the spot where the dress comes to. Her facial expression is dumbfounded: open mouth and wide-eyed as she puts her hand on her forehead. Notice that Wanda doesn't sign any dialogue, only action.

You can use Constructed Action for any type of information — humorous, serious, or simply informative. As with Constructed Dialogue, Constructed Action takes some practice, but it will sharpen your signing prowess.

Chapter 4

Getting Your Numbers and Times Straight

N umbers are a big part of American Sign Language. This chapter gives you the lowdown on using numbers in all kinds of ways. We also cover expressions of time, which come up in conversation all the . . . time (see what we mean?). If you familiarize yourself with the various signs for numbers and time words, you'll be better able to converse with Deaf people, and they'll be impressed with your ability to use these signs in many different types of sentences.

Counting on Numbers

Did you know that you can count in ASL in 27 different ways? That's a pretty cool piece of trivia, but for this book, we concentrate on just two of those ways — cardinal numbers and ordinal numbers. If you'd like to check out some other ways to count, Gallaudet University and the National Technical Institute of the Deaf are great resources.

Cardinal (counting) and ordinal (ordering) numbers will get you through everyday situations, such as counting the millions you won on the lottery, giving your address and phone number to the movie star who wants to get to know you better, and telling your mom that you won the first Pulitzer Prize in your family.

TIP

When you want to specify more than one item — that is, express a plural — you sign the item first, followed by the quantity. Unlike English, you don't have to change the item to a plural by adding "s." A good way to remember this is to keep in mind that you need to show what the item is before you can tell someone how many items there are. For example:

English: Two books
Sign: BOOK TWO

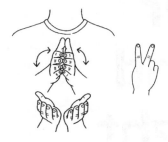

English: Four cars
Sign: CAR FOUR

TIP

To count as you're going through a list, whether you're using ordinal or cardinal numbers, notice whether the list goes straight down or in a row. Follow the pattern in the list when you sign; just count with a small motion either sideways or downward. This is extra information that allows your viewer to see the organization of the list.

Getting from one to ten with cardinal numbers

Being able to give numerical information in ASL opens many doors. You can give someone your phone number, make an appointment, and warn a potential guest that you have 12 — yes 12! — cats and two angry neighbors.

REMEMBER

When you're indicating quantity and counting things, sign the numbers 1 through 5 and 11 through 15 with your palm facing you and the numbers 6 through 10 and 16 through 19 with your palm facing the person to whom you're signing.

Just as in English, there are exceptions to every rule, especially the one about which way your palm faces. To tell time in Sign, let your dominant (active) index finger touch your other wrist in the place where you'd wear a watch, and then use your dominant hand to sign the appropriate hour (number), with your palm facing toward the person you're signing (see the later section "Talking about Time" for more on signing time expressions). The same palm-facing-outward rule applies to addresses and phone numbers (see "Signing phone numbers and the like," later in the chapter).

Table 4-1 shows you how to sign the cardinal numbers 1 through 19.

TABLE 4-1 ## Cardinal Numbers

English	Sign	English	Sign
ONE		TWO	
THREE		FOUR	
FIVE		SIX	

(continued)

TABLE 4-1 *(continued)*

English	Sign	English	Sign
SEVEN		EIGHT	
NINE		TEN	
ELEVEN		TWELVE	
THIRTEEN		FOURTEEN	
FIFTEEN		SIXTEEN	
SEVENTEEN		EIGHTEEN	
NINETEEN			

To sign decade numbers — 30, 40, 50, and so on — you sign the first number (3, 4, 5) followed by the sign for the number **0.** You sign hundreds — such as 600, 700, 800, and so on — by first signing the number (6, 7, 8) and then the sign for **hundred,** as the following examples show:

THIRTY (30)

FORTY (40)

FIFTY (50)

SIX HUNDRED (600)

SEVEN HUNDRED (700)

EIGHT HUNDRED (800)

Ordering ordinal numbers

Ordinal numbers show orderly placement: first cup of coffee, second chapter, and third base, for example. To indicate an ordinal number in ASL, twist your wrist inward while signing the respective number.

FIRST

SECOND

THIRD

Signing phone numbers and the like

As you meet more Deaf people and give out your phone number, sign the numbers with your palm facing outward, toward the person to whom you're giving the information. You'll also encounter some Deaf people who use their index fingers to sign *parenthesis* before signing an area code. Doing so does make the information clearer.

You sign Social Security numbers like phone numbers, with your palm facing the addressee.

Talking about Time

In ASL, telling time can be an important tool to make sure that you're never too late or too early. As you're learning this valuable piece of information, always remember that you should put the expression of time as close to the beginning of the sentence as possible; that is, you generally express the time before the subject. This part of a sentence in ASL allows the Deaf person with whom you're conversing to get a clear concept of when the event happened, effectively framing the information that you're about to share. If you forget to state the time factor early in the sentence, just add it when you can.

The time factor can be a date, a day, a month, "now," "dawn," "tomorrow," "immediately," and so on. However, at this *time*, the *idea* of "when" can be as simple as pointing to your watch and then expressing any given hour. If you want to say that something happened in the morning, sign **morning.** If you want to express nighttime, sign **evening.**

The signs in Table 4-2 help you express time. "Seconds" doesn't have a sign, but if you spell S-E-C after a number, your point will be clear — for example, **three S-E-C.** You sign the following time expressions with two signs: First touch your wrist to indicate a watch/time and then sign the number. Keep your hand with your palm facing outward and you'll be as clear as Big Ben on a sunny day!

TABLE 4-2 ## Time Signs

English	Sign	English	Sign
ONE O'CLOCK	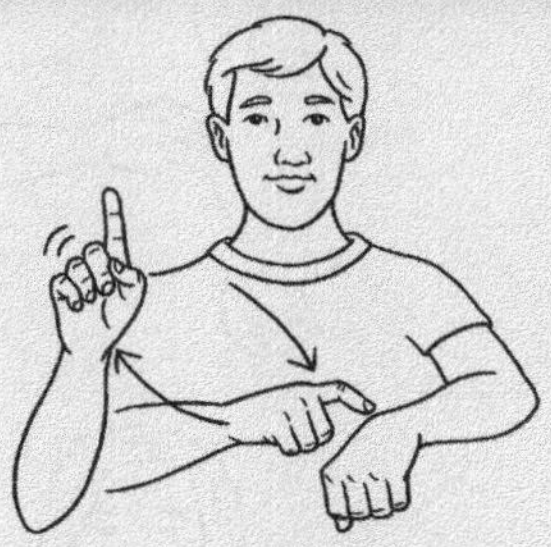	TWO O'CLOCK	
FOUR HOURS	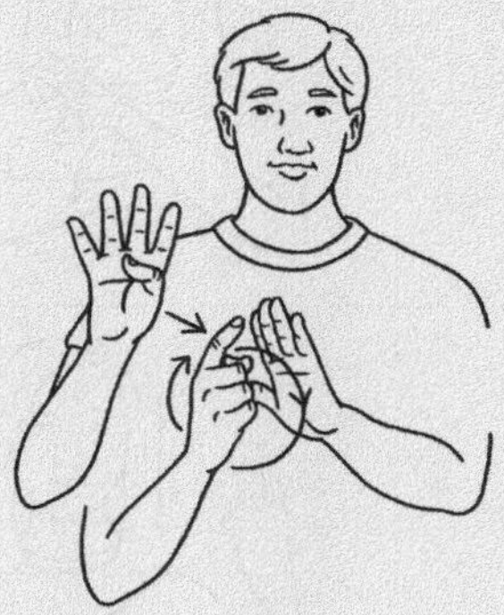	FOUR HOURS (variation)	
TWO MINUTES		TEN MINUTES	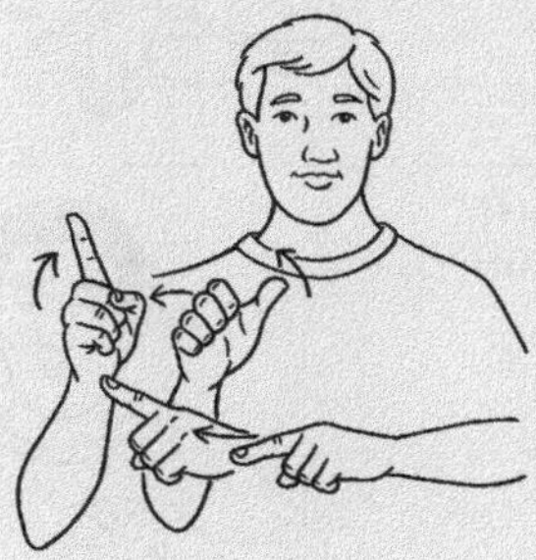

(continued)

TABLE 4-2 *(continued)*

English	Sign	English	Sign
DAWN		MORNING	
NOON		TWILIGHT	
NIGHT		DAY	
ALL NIGHT/ OVERNIGHT		ARRIVE	

English	Sign	English	Sign
SHOW UP		LEAVE (formal)	
LEAVE (informal)		STAY	
ON THE DOT			

Signing calendar dates

We're all slaves to our day planners and schedules, and the Deaf are no different. They rely on their calendars like everyone else. To sign months of the year in ASL, you fingerspell them. You may see a person signing **calendar** while using the first letter of the month incorporated in the sign. This can get confusing because three months start with the letter "J," two start with the letter "M," and two start with the letter "A." This method isn't uncommon, but it's not formal signing either. Until you get your feet under you, fingerspell the months of the year.

Here are a couple of examples:

J-A-N 22, 2022

Here you fingerspell each letter of the month, sign 22, and then sign 2, 0, and 22.

REMEMBER

When two numbers are the same, point your palm downward facing the ground and then sign the number from one side to the other.

N-O-V 17, 2022

Again, fingerspell the month, sign 17, then sign 2, 0, and 22.

REMEMBER

The months that you can abbreviate are Jan., Feb., Aug., Sept., Oct., Nov., and Dec.

The months that you should completely spell out are March, April, May, June, and July.

.... Signin' the Sign ....

Ted is going to Della's house for a visit. Della is giving Ted directions in hopes that he'll arrive on time.

Della:	Can you come over to my house at 7 P.M.?
Sign:	7 P.M. — MY HOUSE — COME — CAN YOU — Q

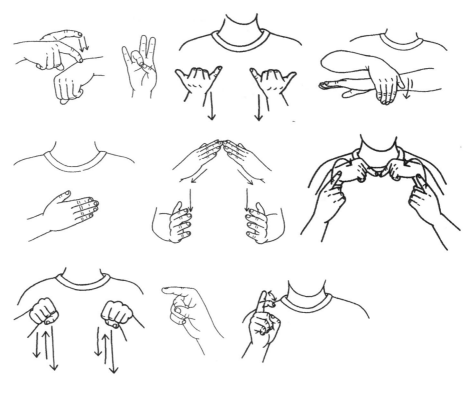

Ted: Yes, I can.
Sign: YES — CAN ME

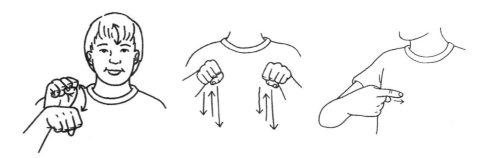

Della: Remember, it's 329 West Drive.
Sign: REMEMBER — HOUSE — WEST — D-R — 3-2-9

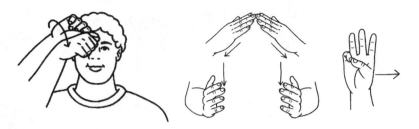

Ted: Can you give me directions?
Sign: DIRECTIONS — GIVE ME — CAN — Q

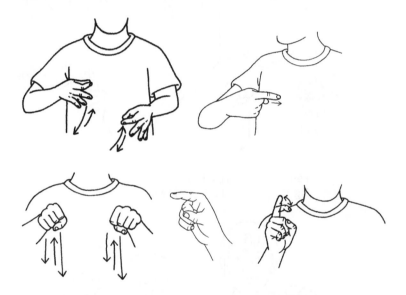

Della: Right on West Drive; the third house on the right.
Sign: HOUSE — THIRD RIGHT — STREET — WEST — D- R

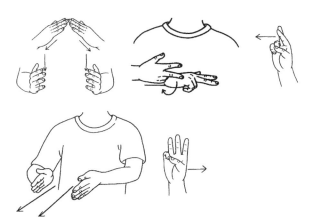

· ·

Chapter 5
Signing at Home

I n this chapter you find things all around the house to identify using American Sign Language. As you go about your house, try to sign as many items as you can as you move from room to room. When you feel you've conquered several rooms, start stringing the signs into short sentences. Later in the chapter, you discover signs for holidays and signs to help you communicate with children.

Handling Signs about Your Home

You can give guests the grand tour of your home without uttering a sound. Notice how the signs in Table 5-1 let your fingers do the talking.

TABLE 5-1 **Dwelling Signs**

English	Sign	English	Sign
DOOR		FLOOR	

(continued)

TABLE 5-1 *(continued)*

English	Sign	English	Sign
GARAGE		HOME	
HOUSE		LIVE	
LOCK		OWN	
RENT		WINDOW	

English	Sign	English	Sign
YARD		UPSTAIRS	
DOWNSTAIRS			

TIP

To sign **condo,** you fingerspell C-O-N-D-O, and to sign **apartment,** you use the abbreviation and fingerspell just A-P-T.

English: Do you own your home or rent?
Sign: YOUR HOME — OWN — RENT WHICH Q

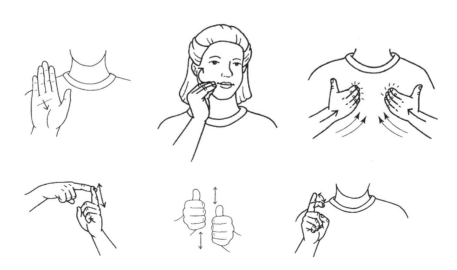

English: The door is locked.
Sign: DOOR — LOCKED

English: The garage has a window.
Sign: GARAGE — WINDOW HAVE

 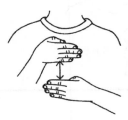

English: His house is big.
Sign: HIS HOUSE — BIG

 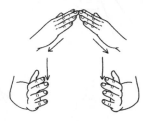 

English: Can I go upstairs?
Sign: UPSTAIRS — GO ME CAN Q

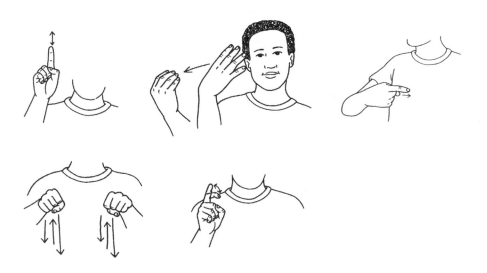

Touring all the rooms

Touring a house room by room yields many surprises. One surprise is that each room has its own sign. (Well, maybe that's not so surprising.) Table 5-2 gives most of them.

TIP

The sign for **closet** has several motions, so here's some explanation: With your dominant hand, make a hook with your index finger. This finger acts as a hanger. Your passive index finger acts as a pole on which to put the hangers. Put several "hangers" onto the "pole."

TABLE 5-2 Rooms

English	Sign	English	Sign
BASEMENT		BATHROOM	
BEDROOM		CLOSET	
DINING ROOM		KITCHEN	
LIVING ROOM			

To get the attention of a Deaf person in a room you're entering, flick the light off and on — that will do the trick.

English: Can I use the bathroom?
Sign: BATHROOM — USE ME CAN Q

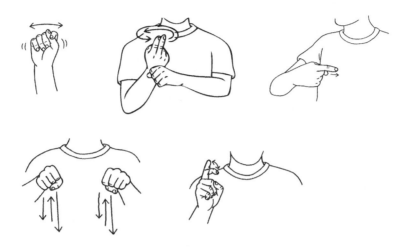

English: Is this your bedroom?
Sign: BEDROOM — YOURS Q

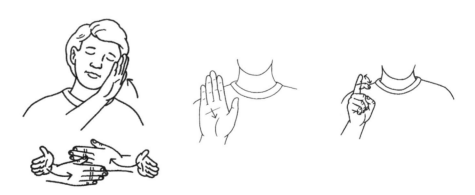

English: The kitchen is hot.
Sign: KITCHEN — HOT

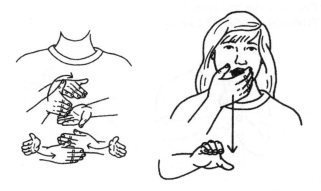

English: Don't play in the living room.
Sign: LIVING ROOM — PLAY THERE — DON'T

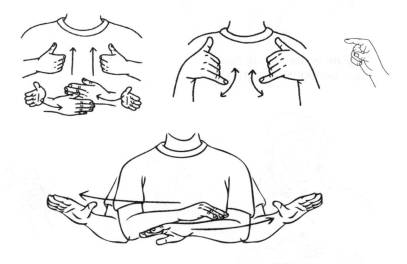

Furnishing your home

After you have rooms, you can start filling them with furniture. Table 5-3 shows you the signs for everything from window treatments to carpet.

TIP

After you have the sign for **chair** down, you'll have no problem with **love seat** or **couch.** To sign **love seat,** sign chair (double motion), and then, with the same handshape, put your dominant hand next to your passive hand to show a couch for two. To sign **couch,** make the sign for chair (single motion), and then move your dominant hand outward to show several seats.

TABLE 5-3 ## Home Furnishings

English	Sign	English	Sign
BED		BLINDS	
CARPET		CHAIR	
COUCH		CURTAINS	

(continued)

TABLE 5-3 *(continued)*

English	Sign	English	Sign
LAMP		LOVE SEAT	
PICTURES		RECLINER	
TABLE		VASE	

If you're comfortable with these furnishings, try the following sentences.

English: Sit on the couch.
Sign: COUCH — SIT

English: Turn on the lamp.
Sign: LAMP O-N

English: My carpet is white.
Sign: MY CARPET — WHITE

English: The picture is pretty.
Sign: PICTURE — PRETTY

Signin' the Sign

 Dave and Debbie have just purchased their first house. Here's what they have to say about it.

Dave: The house has a big yard.
Sign: HOUSE YARD — BIG

Debbie: I want to see the kitchen.
Sign: KITCHEN — WANT SEE ME

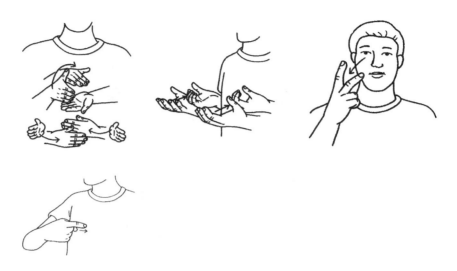

Dave: We need a couch, lamp, and pictures.
Sign: COUCH LAMP PICTURES — NEED US

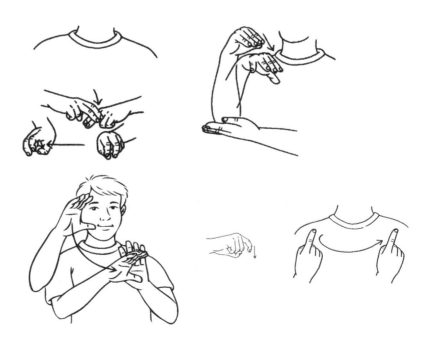

Debbie: It's great to own, not rent, a house.
Sign:　　HOUSE — OWN GREAT — RENT NOT

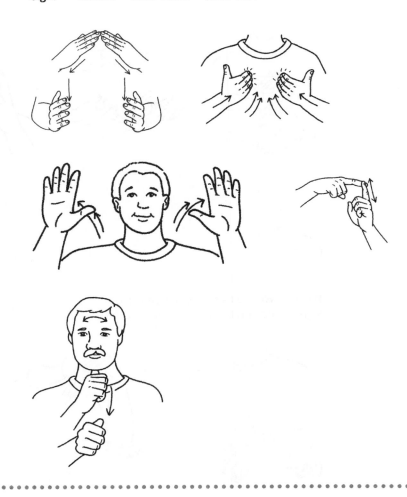

Hanging Out for the Holidays

The holidays and other yearly celebrations are an enjoyable time for family and friends to gather 'round and join in the festive good cheer. Partake in the festivities with your Deaf friends by practicing the signs in Table 5-4.

TIP

If you're gathered around a table with some Deaf folks and you want to propose a toast, knock on the table to create a vibration. You will then have the floor.

TABLE 5-4   Holiday Signs

English	Sign	English	Sign
CHRISTMAS		EASTER	
VALENTINE'S DAY		THANKSGIVING	
MOTHER'S DAY		FATHER'S DAY	

(continued)

TABLE 5-4 *(continued)*

English	Sign	English	Sign
NEW YEAR'S		MEMORIAL DAY	
HALLOWEEN		INDEPENDENCE DAY	
HOLIDAY		CELEBRATION	

Teaching the Tots

Raising a brood is quite a responsibility. Nothing is more impressive than teaching your children a second language like ASL. You can use the signs in Table 5-5 every day around the house. As you're hanging out with your Deaf chums, see which signs they use with their children and take note. These signs have to do with everyday life of the family, whether Deaf or hearing.

TABLE 5-5   **Signs for Children and Family**

English	Sign	English	Sign
SLEEP		DREAM	
REST		PRAY	

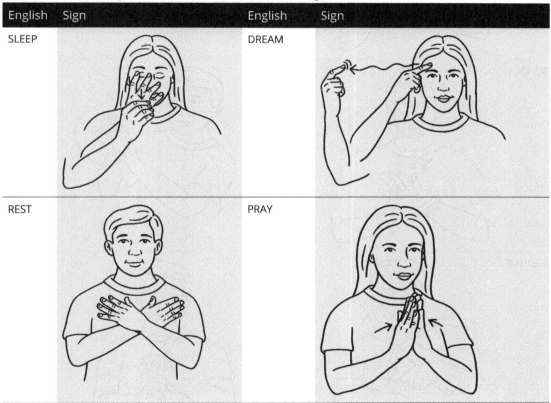

(continued)

TABLE 5-5 *(continued)*

English	Sign	English	Sign
LAUGH		VACATION	
SCHOOL		COLLEGE	
BEDTIME		CHORES	

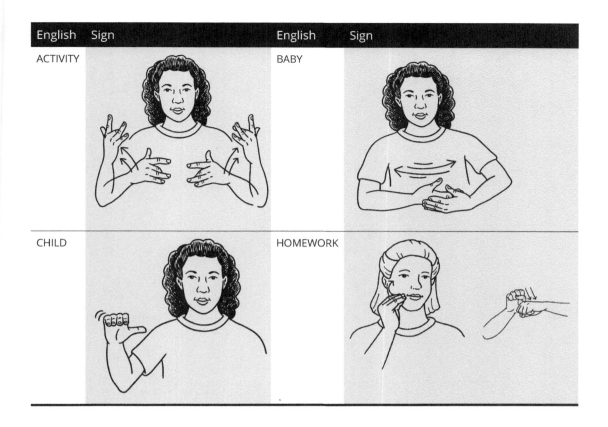

ACTIVITY BABY CHILD HOMEWORK

Keeping Track of Your Subjects in Space

At home or out and about, you often talk about people who aren't right there with you. For instance, at work, you may discuss with one of your co-workers how much you like your boss. When using Sign, you don't have to be able to see someone (or something) to be able to talk about him, her, or it. (That's a good thing, too. How else could you plan a surprise party for your spouse?)

REMEMBER

All you have to do to discuss someone who isn't physically present is assign that person a point in the space near your passive hand. You use the same sign for **he, she,** and **it** — your index finger extended in a pointing gesture (see Chapter 1). If the he, she, or it is nearby, you point your index finger at the person or thing, but if the person or thing isn't in your general vicinity, you select a specific place in the space in front of you to sort of stand in for the person or thing. In ASL, this sign isn't gender-specific. You point to the same space every time you refer to the absent one. So if you want to sign about Buddy, fingerspell his name and point to your passive hand area.

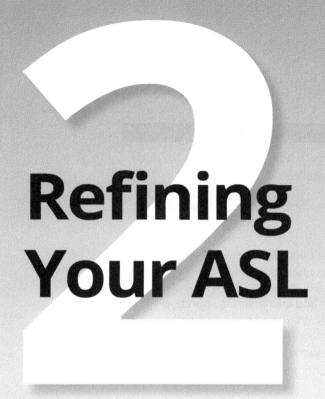

Refining Your ASL

Chapter 6

Asking Questions and Making Small Talk

earing people get to know one another by asking questions and making small talk. Deaf people are no different. You begin with the basics and build from there. This chapter gets you started conversing with your family and friends in American Sign Language by giving you the signs for various information-seeking questions. Then we cover signs for family relationships and signs to help you talk about where you live and work. Finally, we show you the signs for pronouns, including possessives.

Signing Key Questions: Six Ws, One H

When you want to sign a question, you simply put the question word at the end of the sentence — words such as **who, what, when, where, which, why,** and **how.** In this section, we explain these key signs and then show you how to ask questions. As a rule, after you sign your question, you repeatedly sign the manual question mark, which is shown here:

Question mark (end of sentence)

TIP

Throughout this book, the letter **Q** follows all ASL examples and dialogues that are questions. Use the end-of-sentence manual question mark when you see the letter Q in this book.

You also have the option of placing the question mark at the beginning of the sentence:

Question mark (beginning of sentence)

TIP

As you sign the question word, lean forward a little, look inquisitive, scrunch your eyebrows together, and tilt your head to one side.

Your dominant hand — the one that you write with — does the action.

REMEMBER

Always maintain eye contact. That way, you and the other person can make sure that you understand each other.

You sign the following inquiry words at the beginning or at the end of a sentence:

Who? With your dominant hand, place your thumb on your chin and let your index finger wiggle from the joint. The other three fingers curl under.

What? Put your hands outward in front of you, with elbows bent and palms up. Shake your hands back and forth towards each other.

Where? Hold up the index finger of your dominant hand as if you're indicating "number one" and shake it side to side.

When? Put both of your index fingers together at a 90-degree angle at the tips. Your dominant index finger then makes a full circle around the passive index finger and returns to the starting position.

Which? Make both hands into fists with your thumbs pointing up; alternate each fist in an up-and-down movement.

Why? With your dominant hand, palm facing up, bend and wiggle the middle finger. Make this sign close to your temple.

How? With your fingers pointing downward and the backs of your fingers and knuckles touching, roll your hands inward to your chest and up so that the pinky sides of your hands are touching.

Check out the following examples of short questions:

English: Who is going?
Sign: GOING — WHO Q

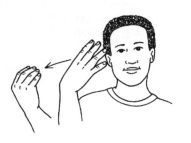  

English: What do you mean?
Sign: MEAN — WHAT Q (the word "you" is implied because you're talking to that person already)

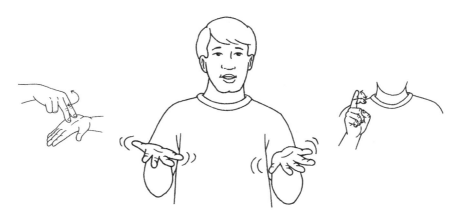

Signin' the Sign

 Virginia and Mark are roommates. It's Saturday morning, and they're drinking coffee and signing about what they have planned for the day.

Mark: Are you working today?
Sign: TODAY — WORKING YOU Q

 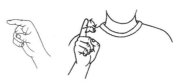

Virginia: Yes, for two hours.

Sign: YES — TWO HOURS — SHORT (this signed answer can be translated to mean, "I am only working briefly")

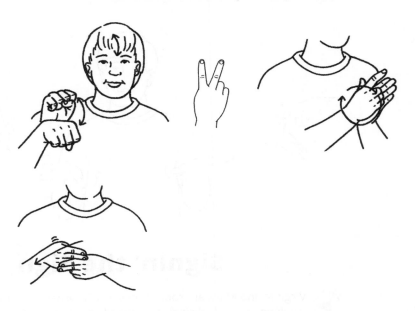

Mark: I'm going to the movies.

Sign: MOVIES — GO ME

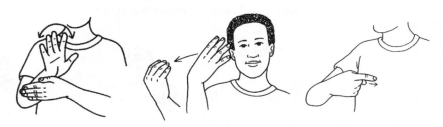

Virginia: May I join you?
Sign: YOU — ME Q

Mark: Of course.
Sign: OF COURSE

....

Discussing Family, Friends, and More

This section helps you confidently share information about yourself and your family. Understanding another person's signs is one thing, but responding to them is another. You already know all the ins and outs of who your relatives are and where you live and work, so here's where you find the most commonly used signs to convey that information.

Family and friends

Describing your family is one way to tell someone about yourself. Using the common signs in Table 6-1 can make your eccentric family seem almost normal.

TABLE 6-1 Family Members

English	Sign	English	Sign
FATHER		MOTHER	
SON		DAUGHTER	
BROTHER		SISTER	

English	Sign	English	Sign
AUNT		UNCLE	
MALE COUSIN		FEMALE COUSIN	
FAMILY		CHILDREN	

TIP

To sign a male cousin or male nephew by your temple, form a manual **C** by your temple and shake it or an **N** and twist it. The same can be done by the jaw to indicate a female cousin or niece. Your hand should never touch your head.

Signs for some other members of your family, such as grandchildren and in-laws, are a bit trickier. To talk about your **grandchildren,** fingerspell G-R-A-N-D and then sign children.

For **in-laws,** sign the person and then sign **law.**

To sign **stepbrother, stepsister, stepfather,** or **stepmother,** sign the letter "L," thumb pointing upward and index finger pointing forward, and shake the hand subtly.

Sign a **half sibling** by expressing the manual ½ and then signing **brother** or **sister.**

Take a look at these examples:

English: Is she your sister?
Sign: (point) HER— SISTER — YOURS Q

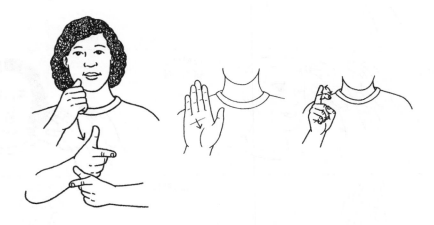

English: No, my sister-in-law.
Sign: NO — SISTER LAW — MINE

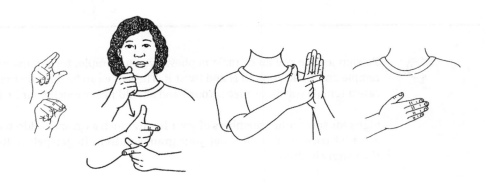

English: He is my half brother.
Sign: MY 1-2 (as in ½) BROTHER — HIM (point)

TIP

To show "½" the palm must be facing the signer, and the 1 then moves in a downward motion (toward the ground) as you pop out your middle finger to join your already raised index finger making the 1 a 2 and, therefore, showing the over-under aspect of ½.

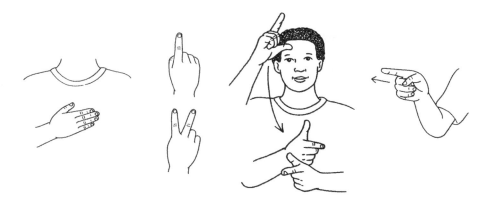

To sign a school friend or work colleague, simply sign the word and then sign **friend.** You may signify a close friend by signing **friend** with more intensity. You can also indicate that close friends are **like two peas in a pod** by signing crossed fingers and pursing your lips; this sign looks the same as when you cross your fingers to mean "good luck" or "I hope so."

Relating where you live and work

Giving others information about your workplace and home is easy — the information is already in your memory. Signing this info to others is a snap, but be careful because many other eyes can see what you sign.

Giving addresses and phone numbers

Exchanging addresses and phone numbers is a great way to make friends with other signers. Asking someone to repeat the information is okay; everyone does it in both English and Sign. You fingerspell most of this information, although the directional words "north," "south," "east," and "west" do have signs (see Chapter 7).

Here are some common abbreviations:

>> **Avenue:** A-V-E

>> **Circle:** C-I-R

>> **Drive:** D-R

>> **Street:** S-T

>> **Apartment:** A-P-T

>> **Way:** W-Y

You sign street addresses by fingerspelling the street name and then signing the house number, keeping your palm facing the addressee. Sign the city's name next, but only when you're sure that the addressee understands the sign.

Prominent cities may have name signs (refer to Chapter 3 for some examples). For less prominent cities, fingerspell the name. Deaf people will show you a local sign if it exists. Often, you sign cities that have two-word names by using the first letter of each word. As a general rule, sign cities the way the Deaf do. As they say, when in Rome. . . .

You sign zip codes with your palm facing outward. Sign all five numbers in succession.

When you sign phone numbers, all numbers face the addressee — outward. If you're not sure that the information you're giving is clear, sign an area code by making parentheses with both index fingers and then sign the numbers. Alternatively, just sign L-D (for long distance) before you give the number.

Signing the suffix part of phone numbers doesn't follow any set rule. Some people fingerspell all four numbers in succession, and others break up the phone number suffix into two sets of two numbers. For instance, if the last four numbers of a phone number are 1212, you can sign them as 1, 2, 1, 2 or 12, 12. You don't need to worry about putting a hyphen between the numbers like you would if you were writing the number down.

The signs in Table 6-2 may help you, too.

TABLE 6-2   **Signs about Where You Live**

English	Sign	English	Sign
DOWNTOWN		COUNTRY	
CITY		TOWN	
STREET		PHONE	
LONG DISTANCE/L-D		ADDRESS	

Signin' the Sign

Donna is moving to Chicago. Mike is hoping that the two of them can stay in touch; Donna feels the same way. Mike wants to get her new address so that he can write to her.

Mike: Where are you moving?
Sign: MOVING YOU — WHERE Q

Donna: Chicago. Will you write?
Sign: CHICAGO — LETTER — WRITE — ME — YOU Q

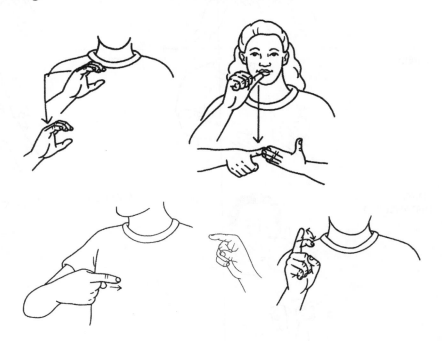

Mike: Yes, what's your address?

Sign: YES — ADDRESS YOURS — WHAT Q

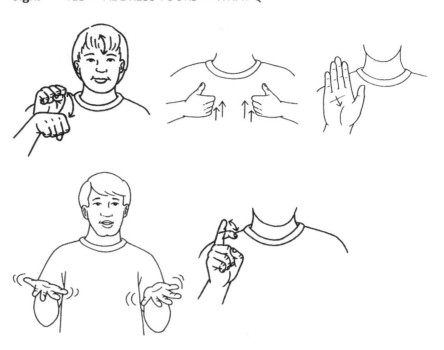

Donna: 171 Anywhere Lane, 98765.

Sign: 1-7-1 A-N-Y-W-H-E-R-E L-A-N-E 9-8-7-6-5

Mike: Thanks. Phone me when you arrive.
Sign: THANKS — ARRIVE YOU — PHONE ME

Jabbering about your job

When you want to tell someone where you work, you usually do it by fingerspelling. If the name of your company is an acronym, you fingerspell that as well. Few places have name signs that are understood by everyone. However, when sharing info about your profession, be it your job title or what your job entails, you can usually use signs. Table 6-3 lists just a few of the many job signs used today.

TABLE 6-3 **Job Signs**

English	Sign	English	Sign
BOSS		COOK	
INTERPRETER		MANAGER	
DOCTOR		ACCOUNTANT	

(continued)

TABLE 6-3 *(continued)*

English	Sign	English	Sign
POLICE		TEACHER	
PRESIDENT		TREASURER	
SECRETARY		VICE PRESIDENT	

English	Sign	English	Sign
MECHANIC		SALESPERSON	
ASSISTANT		LAWYER	
SERVER		PHARMACIST	

All vice presidents are signed V-P by the side of the head, regardless of whether you're talkng about the vice president of the United States or the vice president of the local PTA chapter.

Signin' the Sign

 Juanita and Kim are seated next to each other at a dinner party hosted by Tom, a mutual friend. They strike up a casual conversation.

Kim: Hi, I'm Kim, Tom's accountant.
Sign: HI — K-I-M ME — ACCOUNTANT FOR T-O-M

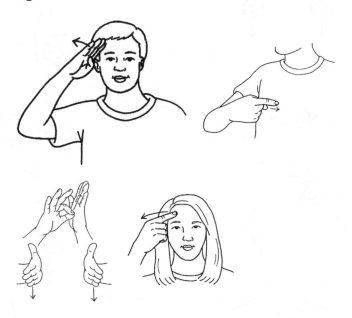

Juanita: I'm Juanita. Nice to meet you.
Sign: J-U-A-N-I-T-A ME — NICE MEET YOU

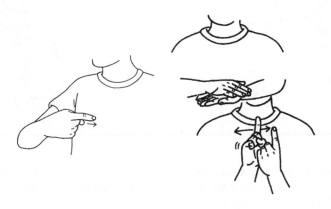

Kim: Do you work at Bailey & Sons?
Sign: B-A-I-L-E-Y S-O-N-S — YOU WORK Q

Juanita: Yes, I'm vice president of marketing.
Sign: YES — MARKETING — V-P — ME

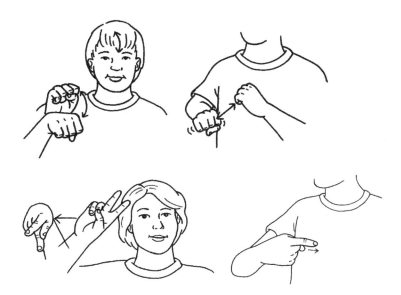

Kim: What an interesting job.
Sign: JOB — INTERESTING — TRUE

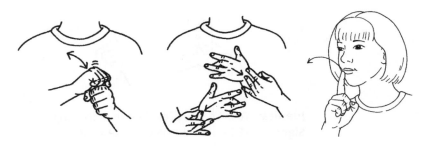

Juanita: I sure meet a lot of different people.
Sign: DIFFERENT — PEOPLE — MEET ME

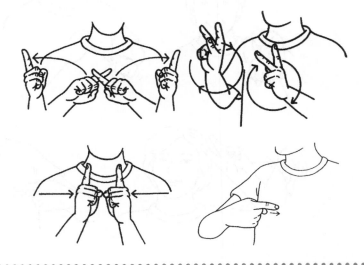

Using Possessives and Pronouns When Chatting

In the course of getting to know someone, or having a mutual acquaintance, when asking each other questions, you'll find that using pronouns is probably easiest. You use pronouns in Sign the same way that you do in English; you need to refer to a noun before you use a pronoun. Of course, if you're using a pronoun to indicate someone or something nearby, you can point to that person or thing as you sign.

You may also use possessives during your conversation. Show possession by indicating whom you're talking about or what's being possessed and then showing an open palm facing the person. You can also use proper nouns (a person's name) to discuss possessives. Fingerspell the name of the person, point to the item you're talking about, and sign a question mark. For example, suppose that you're signing with someone and you want to know if the coat on the hook belongs to Tony. Fingerspell T-O-N-Y, point to the coat, and sign a question mark.

If you're signing *with* Tony, point to the object or fingerspell it if it's not in view, look at Tony, sign toward him with an open palm, and then make a question mark. You've now asked him, "Is that yours?" Remember to keep your eyebrows up and wear an inquisitive look.

Personal pronouns and possessives

Table 6-4 lists pronouns that refer to people and also gives you the signs for the possessive pronouns.

TABLE 6-4   **Personal and Possessive Pronouns**

Pronoun	Sign	Possessive	Sign
I, ME		MY, MINE	

(continued)

TABLE 6-4 *(continued)*

Pronoun	Sign	Possessive	Sign
HE		HIS	
SHE		HERS	
YOU (singular)		YOUR, YOURS (singular)	
YOU (plural)		YOUR, YOURS (plural)	
WE, US		OUR, OURS	

Pronoun	Sign	Possessive	Sign
THEY, THEM		THEIR, THEIRS	
IT		ITS	

As you can see, you use some signs for more than one pronoun. Simple sentences can follow English word order. Put the possessive pronoun sign before or after the person or thing you're signing; the order doesn't matter. For example:

English: My dog.
Sign: DOG MINE or MY DOG

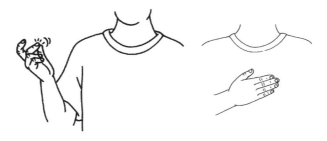

Demonstrative pronouns

As a group, four little pronouns — **this, that, these,** and **those** — get a big name, *demonstrative pronouns.* But you don't really need to know the names, just the signs, which are in Table 6-5.

Pronoun	Sign	Plural	Sign
THIS		THESE	
THAT		THOSE	

TABLE 6-5   **Demonstrative Pronouns**

Sign the pronoun **that** by pointing to your subject with your dominant hand in the **Y** shape and bent at the wrist. Sign **this, these,** and **those** by pointing to the subject or subjects.

Sign singular possessives by holding your hand, palm outward, toward the person to whom you're referring. Sign plural possessives the same way, but also move your hand from side to side in front of each person in a sort of sweeping motion.

The following sentences give you some practice with pronouns and possessives:

English: He is rich.
Sign: RICH HIM

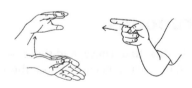

English: He has money.
Sign: MONEY HIS

English: She is wise.
Sign: WISE HER

English: She has wisdom.
Sign: WISDOM HERS

English: They have gold.
Sign: GOLD HAVE THEM

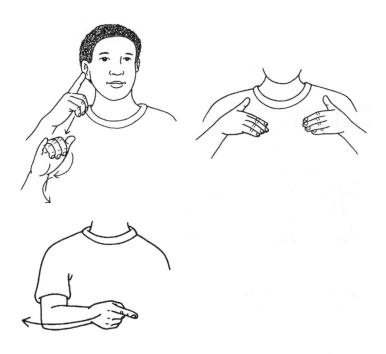

English: The gold is theirs.
Sign: GOLD THEIRS

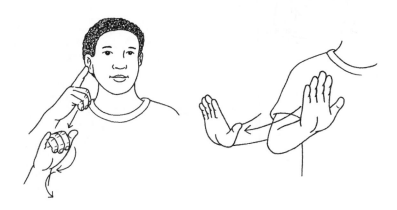

IN THIS CHAPTER

Giving and getting directions in Sign

Making use of natural and urban landmarks in your directions

Using signs for transportation

Adding conjunctions to your directions

Chapter 7
Asking for Directions

G etting where you need to go can happen as quickly as a wave of your hand. You can go a long way by using the signs for directions and transportation that are included in this chapter.

Finding Your Way

REMEMBER

When giving or getting directions in American Sign Language, you need to keep two things in mind. Get these strategies down and you can tell people exactly where to go and how to get there:

>> Try to start with a point of reference that's familiar to both of you, such as a store, restaurant, or bridge, and then give the directions.

>> Go from big to small; from general to specific.

>> For example, in the United States, you go from state to city to neighborhood to street to house number.

Table 7-1 groups signs for compass points and other directional signals. Notice that the handshapes you use for the **compass points** and for **left** and **right** are the first letters of the words.

TABLE 7-1   **Compass Points**

English	Sign	English	Sign
NORTH		SOUTH	
EAST		WEST	
LEFT		RIGHT	

The following examples show you how to sign directions in perfect order.

English: My house is west of the store.
Sign: STORE — MY HOUSE — WEST

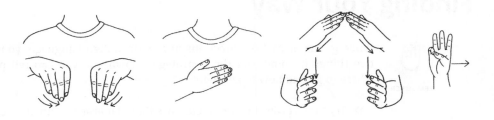

English: Turn right twice.
Sign: RIGHT — RIGHT

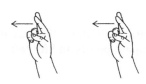

Notice that you don't sign the word *twice*; you simply sign **right** twice. Make sure you shift your body ever so slightly as you start to sign **right** the second time.

To give directions, you often establish relationships. Don't worry; you don't have to commit for very long. Table 7-2 lists the signs for the situational relationships you use to give directions as well as some landmarks and distances that you might use.

TIP

To sign **straight,** use the B manual handshape and then move it straight out in front of you, bending your wrist.

The sign for **straight** is also one sign for **sober** — the sentence's context tells you which word is being signed. Also, you use this same B handshape to sign the direction to turn left or right onto a street. Some people use the sign for **left** or **right** before this B sign. In many cases, it adds clarification.

TABLE 7-2   ## Directional Relationship Signs

English	Sign	English	Sign
AFTER		BACK	
BEFORE		BEHIND	
BESIDE		CROSS STREET/ INTERSECTION	

(continued)

TABLE 7-2 *(continued)*

English	Sign	English	Sign
FORWARD		IN FRONT OF	
STRAIGHT		TURN	
NEAR		FAR	

The following sentences put these signs in action.

English: Go straight; don't turn.
Sign: STRAIGHT — TURN — DON'T

English: The cross street is Maple Drive.
Sign: CROSS STREET WHAT — M-A-P-L-E D-R

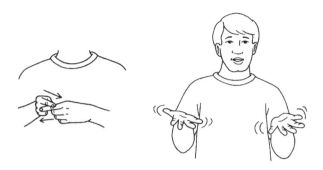

Signin' the Sign

 Buddy is going to the mall. Although he knows the town of Pueblo, he isn't sure how to get to the mall from where he's located. He sees Linda; she knows the town well. Notice how she helps him while using a familiar reference point.

Buddy: How do I get to the mall?
Sign: M-A-L-L ARRIVE — HOW Q

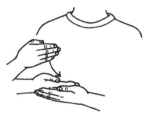 

Linda: Do you know where the museum is?
Sign: MUSEUM WHERE — KNOW YOU Q

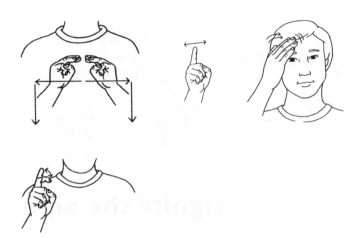

Buddy: From this cross street I go north.
Sign: HERE CROSS STREET — NORTH GO ME

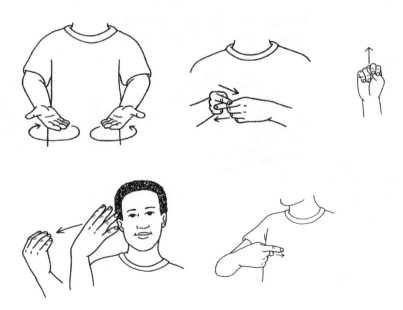

Linda:	Yes, but turn east after two miles.
Sign:	YES — BUT TWO M-I-L-E-S FINISH — GO EAST

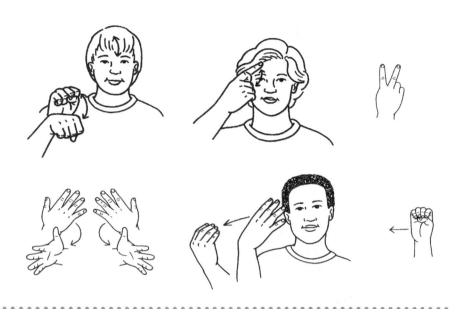

Looking to Natural Landmarks

Most people find landmarks to be helpful when giving or receiving directions. After all, telling someone to turn right at the bottom of the hill is much easier than telling someone to turn right after traveling 1.3 miles. The signs for natural landmarks in Table 7-3 are sure to help you.

TABLE 7-3   **Natural Landmarks**

English	Sign	English	Sign
FIELD		HILL	
LAKE		MOUNTAIN	
RIVER		TREE	

English	Sign	English	Sign
WATERFALL		ROCK/STONE	

TIP

You may see some people fingerspell *field*; whether you fingerspell it or sign it, the goal is to be as clear as possible.

Take a look at the following sentences to see how you can use these landmark signs when giving directions.

English: When you get to the lake, turn right.
Sign: LAKE ARRIVE — RIGHT TURN

REMEMBER

In ASL, you sign **get to** as **arrive.**

English: At the base of the mountain is a small store.
Sign: MOUNTAIN BASE — SMALL STORE — THERE

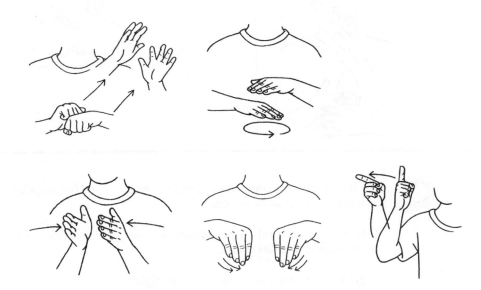

Searching the Streets

Going through town can be overwhelming unless you know how to get where you're going. Table 7-4 demonstrates the landmarks you can use to direct someone in the city.

TIP

You sign **building** with both hands in the H handshape, but don't tuck in your thumbs — leave them out. Place one hand on top of the other four times; then, with B handshapes, palms facing each other, go straight up — go high for a skyscraper.

You sign a **stop sign** by making the sign for **stop** and then making a square-cut line with your index finger. It would be great to make the octagon shape, but who can?

TABLE 7-4 **Urban Landmarks**

English	Sign	English	Sign
BRIDGE		BUILDING	
GAS STATION		HIGHWAY	
ROAD/STREET		STOPLIGHT	

(continued)

TABLE 7-4 *(continued)*

English	Sign		English	Sign
STOP SIGN			MPH	

You've no doubt given directions similar to the ones in the following examples. Now, see how to do it in Sign.

English: Pass the park and go three miles south.
Sign: P-A-R-K PASS — SOUTH THREE M-I-L-E-S GO

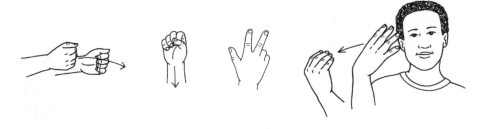

English: At the stop sign, go right.
Sign: STOP SIGN ARRIVE — RIGHT

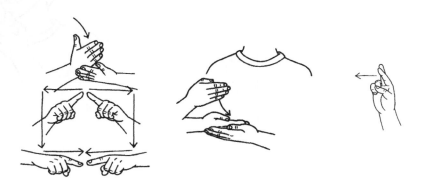

English: Go across the bridge.
Sign: BRIDGE — GO OVER

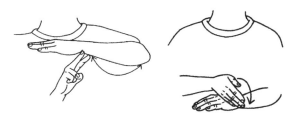

English: The gas station is near the highway.
Sign: HIGHWAY — GAS STATION — NEAR

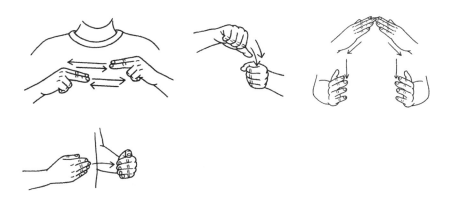

Transporting Yourself

Whether you just need to get around town or you decide to see the world, your travel requires wheels. This section gives you just that. Consider the signs in Table 7-5 for your free-wheeling adventures.

TABLE 7-5   **Wheels**

English	Sign	English	Sign
BICYCLE		CAR	
MOTORCYCLE		PLANE	
SUBWAY		TRAIN	

Bus is fingerspelled B–S — leave out the "u." To sign **driving a bus,** mimic a truck-size steering wheel at the lower chest level, wrap your hands around the imaginary wheel, and steer back and forth. This motion also works for trucks, RVs (after you fingerspell R–V), or any large vehicle. Just fingerspell the big rig first.

Get the wheels in motion, so to speak, by using these automotive signs.

English: The car was in an accident.
Sign: FINISH—CAR—ACCIDENT—HAVE

You sign **accident** by making a 5 handshape, palms facing you, fingertips facing each other. Crash them together, ending in an S handshape.

English: If I miss the train, I'll fly.
Sign: TRAIN MISS — FLY ME — WILL

English: You need a motorcycle helmet.
Sign: MOTORCYCLE HELMET — NEED YOU

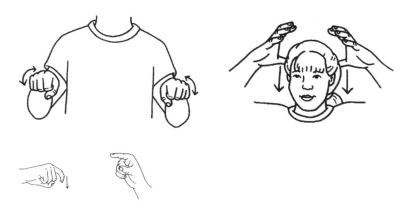

Directing Your Sentences with Conjunctions

As you probably remember from grammar classes of long ago, *conjunctions* join thoughts or phrases. One of the most common conjunctions is *but,* so we explain that one first.

To sign **but,** put your dominant hand on the dominant side of your head and flick your index finger twice, ending with your index finger up.

Check out the following example.

English: Go to the party but be home at midnight.
Sign: PARTY GO — BUT HOME MIDNIGHT — MUST YOU

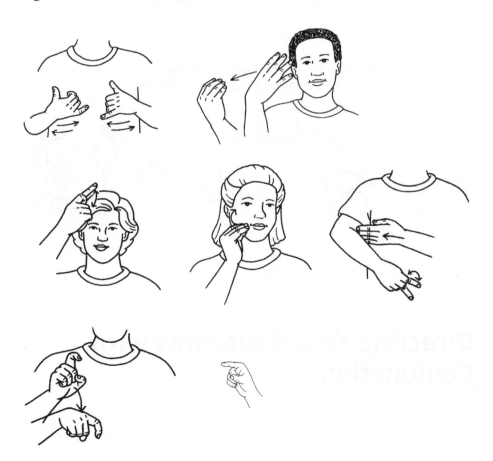

The either/or and neither/nor conjunctions are called *correlative conjunctions*, and you use your hands and head to convey these signs.

REMEMBER

When signing **either . . . or** and **neither . . . nor,** keep in mind that you use these conjunctions to answer these types of questions, not to ask them. So although you don't use the facial expressions you use to ask questions, you keep your head still or nod "yes" for affirmation when you sign **either,** and you shake your head from side to side while signing **neither.**

English: Do you want apples or oranges?
Sign: APPLES ORANGES — WANT YOU — WHICH

English response: Either apples or oranges would be fine.
Sign response: EITHER FINE

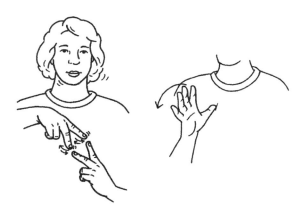

English: Do you want chicken or steak?
Sign: CHICKEN STEAK — WANT YOU — WHICH

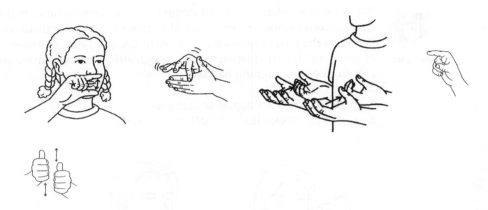

English response: I want neither chicken nor steak.
Sign response: NEITHER

Chapter 8

Dining and Going to the Market

When dining out with Deaf people, who love to wine and dine like anyone else, you may want to ask them what's good on the menu, but perhaps you don't know how. This chapter covers signing three square meals, dining out and ordering drinks, and finding sales and specials in the grocery store.

Eating Three Square Meals a Day

When you're lucky enough to get an invitation to join other signers for brunch, take along these signs to get you through the event. In this part, we will see signs for breakfast, lunch, and dinner, plus everything you'll see on the table — except your elbows. Before you dive into a dish of delights for any meal, check out Table 8-1 for a list of some necessary tools.

TABLE 8-1   **Utensils and Dishes**

English	Sign	English	Sign
BOWL		CUP	
FORK		GLASS (drinking)	
KNIFE		NAPKIN	
PLATE		SPOON	

TIP

These next sentences help you see American Sign Language in action. Here's how to sign the words for what you'll need at the table. A good host knows not only when to use the salad fork but also how to sign it. To sign **place setting**, sign **fork, knife,** and **spoon.** A great way to remember how to make the signs for tableware is pretty simple: what you do with the objects relates to the signs. For example, you sign **napkin** with a wiping motion on the mouth; you sign **spoon** using a scooping motion; you sign **fork** with a stabbing motion; and you sign **knife** using a cutting motion.

English: I need another place setting, please.
Sign: PLEASE — FORK — KNIFE — SPOON — NEED ME

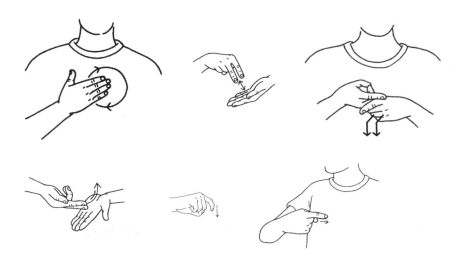

English: The plate and glass are broken.
Sign: PLATE — GLASS — BROKEN

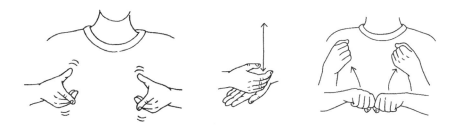

English: I need three bowls.
Sign: THREE BOWLS — NEED ME

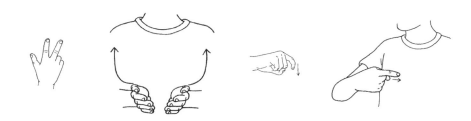

English: The napkin is dirty.
Sign: NAPKIN — DIRTY

Table 8-2 shows you how to sign meal-related words.

TABLE 8-2	Mealtime
English	**Sign**
BREAKFAST	
LUNCH	
DINNER	

English	Sign
FOOD	
EAT	
HUNGRY	
FULL	

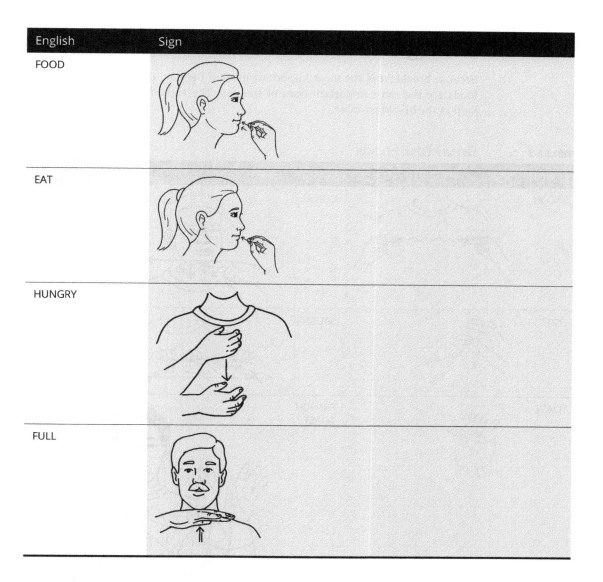

TIP

If you want to show **gorging,** sign **food** with both hands alternately putting food in your mouth while your cheeks are puffed out or your mouth is wide open. The faster you sign, the more you gorge. To sign **starving,** just sign **hungry** faster, open your mouth a little, and look hungry. Don't forget your facial expression. It'll really show just how full or hungry you are! For example, when you sign **full,** use puffed cheeks.

Having breakfast

Because breakfast is the most important meal of the day, the signs for breakfast foods are the most important ones of the day. The signs in Table 8-3 certainly help at the breakfast table.

TABLE 8-3   **Breakfast Foods**

English	Sign	English	Sign
BACON		CEREAL	
EGG		SAUSAGE	
TOAST		FRENCH TOAST	

Even if you're still half asleep, you won't have any problems figuring out most of these signs. The sign for **bacon** mimics the waviness of a fried strip; **toast** lets you know that the bread is browned on both sides; **cereal** is the crunchy stuff you chew. Use the common abbreviations for **orange juice** and sign the letters **O** and **J** to convey this popular breakfast beverage. Get going on practicing your early-morning skills with the following examples:

English: I want eggs, not cereal.
Sign: EGGS WANT — CEREAL NOT — ME

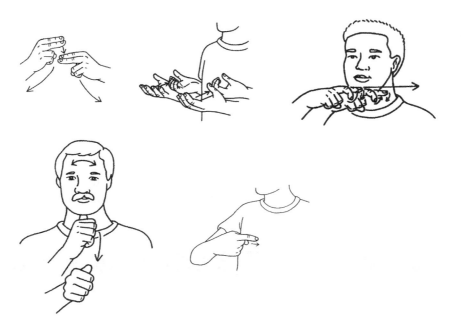

English: The orange juice is cold.
Sign: COLD O-J

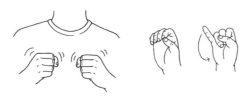

English: I'll have sausage and eggs.
Sign: SAUSAGE — EGGS — HAVE ME

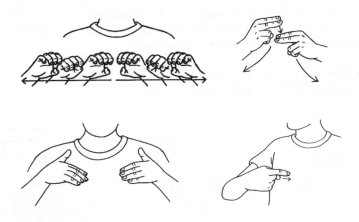

Munching on lunch

Doing lunch with friends is at your fingertips. The set of signs in Table 8-4 can hold you through the afternoon. Just don't get too excited about signing these items or you may end up eating them all in one sitting!

TABLE 8-4   **Lunch Items**

English	Sign	English	Sign
BURGER		CHEESE	

English	Sign	English	Sign
SODA		FRENCH FRIES	
PIZZA		SALAD	
SANDWICH		FRUIT	

To order a hamburger, you imitate the motions of making a patty, but for other lunch signs, you use the manual alphabet. For example, you sign **French fries** by repeating the letter **F** from one side to the other side as if you are dipping them, and you sign **pizza** by bending your index and middle fingers and then making a manual **Z**. (Refer to Chapter 1 to see how to sign the letters of the manual alphabet.) Follow these examples:

English: I'm hungry, and it's time for lunch.
Sign: NOW TIME — NOON FOOD — HUNGRY ME

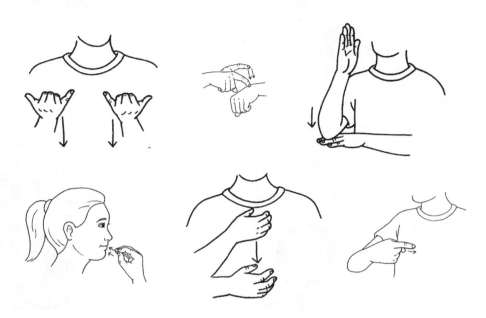

English: I want a cheeseburger and fries.
Sign: CHEESEBURGER — FRIES — WANT — ME

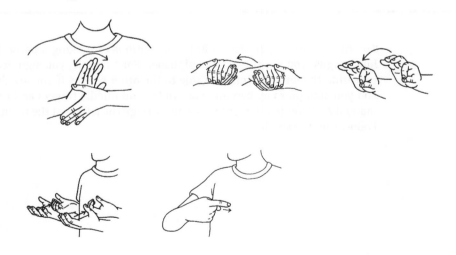

English: The soda is cold.
Sign: SODA — COLD

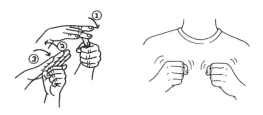

English: I want a sandwich and salad for lunch.
Sign: NOON FOOD — SANDWICH — SALAD — WANT ME

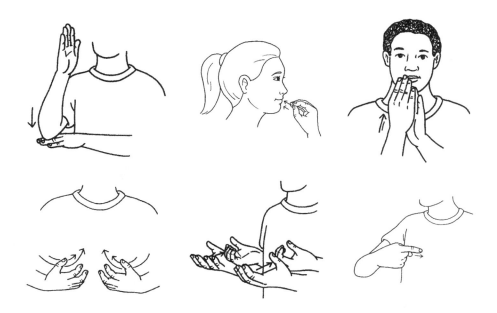

Signin' the Sign

Two co-workers are going to lunch and are discussing what they're in the mood to eat. Here's what they each decide.

Dee: I'm hungry; I want a hamburger, French fries, and a soda.
Sign: HUNGRY ME — HAMBURGER FRENCH FRIES SODA — WANT ME

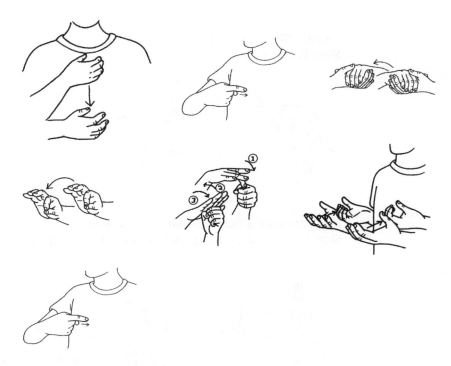

Ted: I want a fish sandwich and water.
Sign: FISH SANDWICH — WATER — WANT ME

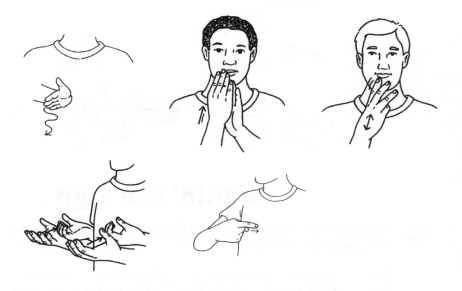

Dee: They have chicken.
Sign: CHICKEN — HAVE THEM (point)

. . . .

Enjoying dinner

Supper is ready, and so are you. Putting the evening meal into conversation is a piece of cake. Follow the signs in Table 8-5 and you'll say a mouthful. (The signs for drinks are coming up in the "Don't forget the drinks!" section.)

TABLE 8-5   **Dinner Terms**

English	Sign	English	Sign
BREAD		CHICKEN	
FISH		CORN	

(continued)

TABLE 8-5 *(continued)*

English	Sign	English	Sign
HAM		POTATO	
SOUP		SPAGHETTI	
STEAK		GRAVY	

Fortunately, you sign **chicken, fish,** and **pig** like the food they provide. If you want to order steak or beef, you can use the same sign for either one.

TIP

Signing how you want it cooked is a breeze; just use the manual alphabet and give your hand a little shake: M for medium, but fingerspell M-E-D W-E-L-L and W-E-L-L. If you want your steak rare, fingerspell R-A-R-E.

WARNING

Don't sign rare with a shaken **R** — the untrained eye could mistake that motion for "restroom" or the direction "right."

Here are some dinner-related sentences to give you practice:

English: Soup and bread were served.
Sign: FINISH — SOUP — BREAD — SERVE

Finish at the beginning of a sentence adds past tense to the whole sentence. (See Chapter 2 for more information on signing in past and future tense.)

English: Chicken and spaghetti are on special.
Sign: SPECIAL — WHAT — CHICKEN — SPAGHETTI

English: The steak is rare.
Sign: STEAK — R-A-R-E

English: I'd like a potato with my fish.
Sign: MY FISH — POTATO TOGETHER — WANT ME

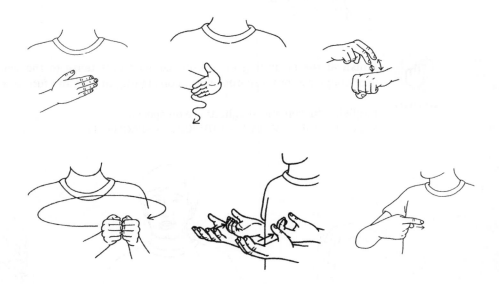

English: I'm full.
Sign: FULL ME

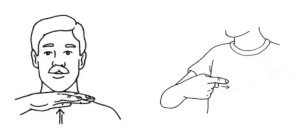

Dining Out

Everyone enjoys going out to restaurants from time to time. Take a look at the signs in Table 8-6, which you can use no matter what type of restaurant you go to. Bon appetit!

REMEMBER

Deaf people usually point out to the server what they want on the menu. If you're dining out with Deaf people, don't try to take control when ordering. They've probably been eating in restaurants long before they met you.

TABLE 8-6   **Words for Dining Out**

English	Sign	English	Sign
ORDER		RESERVATION	
RESTAURANT		SERVER/ WAITER/WAITRESS	

Ethnic food around town

Restaurant row is just down the street. Many Deaf people enjoy eating at ethnic establishments, and I know you'd like to enjoy both the food and the company. The food signs in Table 8-7 are just the thing to get you going — come and get it!

CULTURAL WISDOM

ASL doesn't have established signs for ethnic foods. If the grub is popular, you may see a variety of ways to sign it if there isn't already an established sign from its country of origin. In the southwestern part of the United States, Mexican food is popular, and Mexican Sign Language for this ethnic food is pretty well established in the border states.

TABLE 8-7 **Ethnic Foods**

English	Sign	English	Sign
LASAGNA		SUSHI	
TACO		TORTILLA	
TOSTADA		HUNGARIAN GOULASH	

The following sentences will work up an appetite for any eager signer:

English: We will eat dinner at a restaurant.
Sign: RESTAURANT — EVENING FOOD — EAT THERE — WE WILL

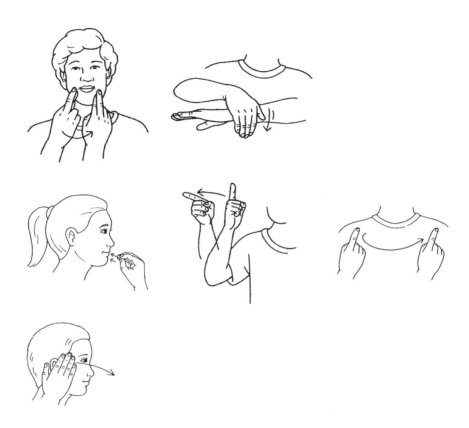

English: I like egg rolls.
Sign: EGG R–O–L–L–S — LIKE ME

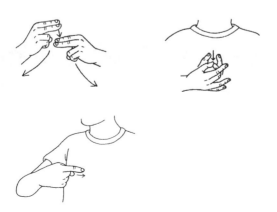

English: Tostadas are cheap.
Sign: TOSTADA — CHEAP

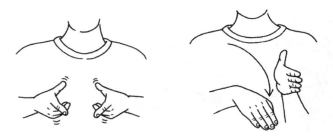

English: She likes tortillas.
Sign: TORTILLAS — SHE LIKES

Don't forget the drinks!

When dining out or going for a night on the town, drinks are often a big part of the occasion. Table 8-8 can help you when ordering common beverages.

TABLE 8-8 **Common Beverages**

English	Sign	English	Sign
BEER		COFFEE	

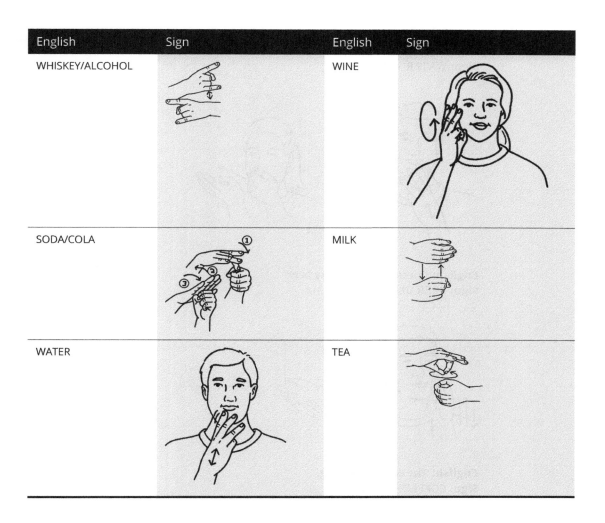

English	Sign	English	Sign
WHISKEY/ALCOHOL		WINE	
SODA/COLA		MILK	
WATER		TEA	

English: We need ice.
Sign: I-C-E — NEED US

 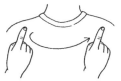

English: The water is warm.
Sign: WATER — WARM

English: I need a glass for my beer.
Sign: BEER GLASS — NEED ME

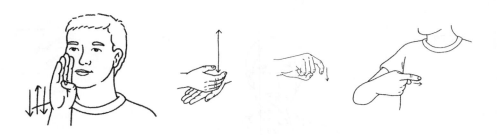

English: The coffee is strong.
Sign: COFFEE — STRONG

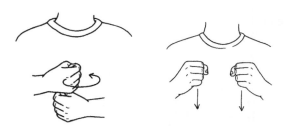

Signin' the Sign

 Belinda and Denni are out on the town. Belinda wants to propose a toast and is asking about drinks when the waitress approaches.

Belinda: What would you like to drink?
Sign: DRINK — WANT WHAT Q

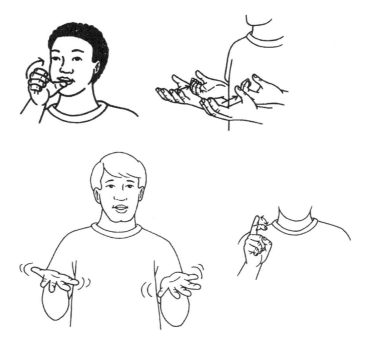

Denni: A cold beer.
Sign: COLD BEER

Belinda: A glass of red wine.
Sign: GLASS RED WINE

Attention, Shoppers!

Grocery shopping made simple — that's what you'll find when you do it in Sign. This section gives you a handle on going to the market and other food-related stores.

Signing specialty stores

Everyone at one time or another goes to the market. You'll be the guru of groceries, hands down, when using the signs from Table 8-9.

TABLE 8-9   **Types of Stores**

English	Sign	English	Sign
BAKERY (BREAD STORE)		BUTCHER (MEAT STORE)	

English	Sign	English	Sign
DISCOUNT STORE		GROCERY (FOOD STORE)	

English: I went to the butcher's.
Sign: FINISH — MEAT STORE — GO ME

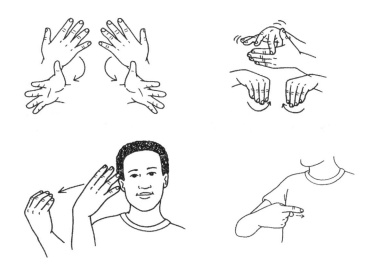

English: The bakery smells good.
Sign: BREAD STORE — SMELLS DELICIOUS

Getting a good deal

Few things are more satisfying than saving money when you're shopping for groceries. Signing specials from the marketplace, like those in Table 8-10, give you the upper hand as you finger your way through the fruit. Note that some signs mean several words, as in "two for the price of one."

TABLE 8-10   **Sale Ad Words**

English	Sign	English	Sign
SAVE		SPEND/BUY	
SELL		BARGAIN/CHEAP	

English	Sign	English	Sign
COUPON		GIFT CARD	

English: The meat is on sale today.
Sign: TODAY — MEAT — SALE

English: You can buy two steaks for the price of one.
Sign: TWO STEAKS — PAY — ONLY ONE

English: I saved money.
Sign: FINISH — MONEY— SAVE ME

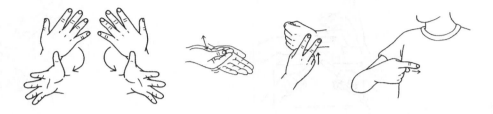

English: You spent too much.
Sign: FINISH — SPEND — (you is implied) TOO MUCH

Chapter 9

Shopping Made Easy

Signing and shopping fit together like hand and glove. This chapter focuses on fashions, colors, and seasons in American Sign Language. We throw in signs for money and comparing prices, too — at no cost to you.

Clothes for All Seasons

Dapper duds are all the rage. These signs show you how to ask for and get your garb in any season because everyone loves a well-dressed signer. Table 9-1 talks fabric. Although you fingerspell many fabrics, here are some fabrics that you sign.

REMEMBER

Fabric signs bear a strong resemblance to what they represent. For example, the sign for **leather** is similar to cowhide, and the **cotton** sign is like tearing apart a cotton ball.

TABLE 9-1   Fabrics

English	Sign	English	Sign
COTTON		FABRIC	
LEATHER		ELASTIC	

These words are the basics for all your clothing needs. You sign **wear** the same way as **use,** so don't worry that they look the same. The sign for **clothes** is the same as the sign for **costume** — try that on for size!

WEAR

CLOTHES

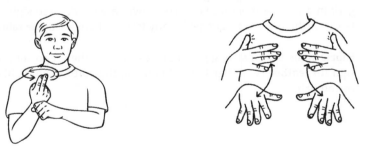

The winter look

Changing with the seasons is no problem. Winter wear signs are cool because they look like what they are. Check them out in Table 9-2.

TABLE 9-2 **Winter Clothing**

English	Sign	English	Sign
BOOTS		COAT	
GLOVES		HAT	
HOODIE		SCARF	

ASL has a variety of signs for gloves because there are different kinds of gloves. Either way, you want to mimic putting on a pair of gloves. You sign **mittens** by making an outline of your thumb and four fingers with the index finger of your passive hand. Mittens aren't as common as gloves, so if people don't understand you, you can always rely on fingerspelling.

TIP

Hat and **scarf** are simple: Sign them like you're putting them on.

Men tend to sign **boots** by mimicking pulling boots on their legs. Women tend to sign boots on the arm. (This isn't a rule, only an observation.)

Try these sentences on for size:

English: Wear your coat.
Sign: YOUR COAT WEAR

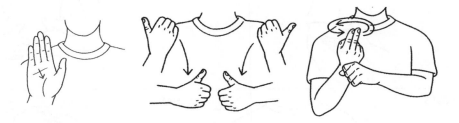

English: The scarf is white.
Sign: SCARF WHITE

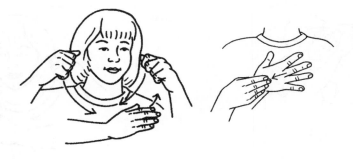

English: Are these your gloves?
Sign: GLOVES YOURS Q

Now, it's time to go undercover. You sign most underwear signs to look like what they represent. You can sign **men's briefs** like **panties**. You may often see **long johns** expressed by signing **long** and then fingerspelling J-O-H-N-S. One way to sign **T-shirt** is with the manual handshape **T** and then **shirt**. You fingerspell anything slinky or kinky. Take a look at Table 9-3 for clarification.

TABLE 9-3   ## Underwear

English	Sign	English	Sign
PANTIES		BRA	
UNDERWEAR (women)		UNDERWEAR (men)	
T-SHIRT			

Fall fashion

You'll have no trouble with fall fashions when you know the basic signs for cool weather wear (see Table 9-4).

TABLE 9-4   **Cool Clothing**

English	Sign	English	Sign
BELT		DRESS	
HIGH HEELS		PANTS/SLACKS	
SHIRT		SHOES	
SOCKS		SWEATER	

Be cool. Practice these sentences that feature cool-weather wear:

English: Your dress is pretty.
Sign: YOUR DRESS — PRETTY

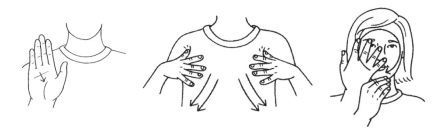

English: Her belt is leather.
Sign: HER BELT — LEATHER

English: If you wear pants, don't wear high heels.
Sign: IF PANTS WEAR — HIGH HEELS WEAR NOT

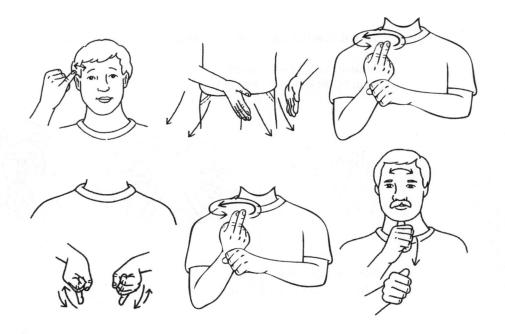

English: Where is my sweater?
Sign: MY SWEATER — WHERE Q

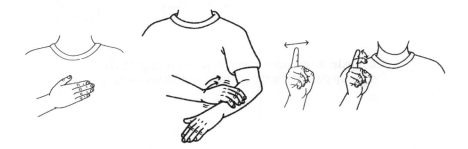

Spring style

Dressing for spring is a beautiful thing. The signs in Table 9-5 show you how to fit in all the fashionable circles when the weather begins to warm up.

TABLE 9-5   Spring Apparel and Accessories

English	Sign	English	Sign
BLOUSE		PURSE	
SKIRT		NYLONS	
TIE		UMBRELLA	
WALLET		BACKPACK	

Spring into action and take a look at the following sentences:

English: Where's my umbrella?
Sign: MY UMBRELLA — WHERE Q

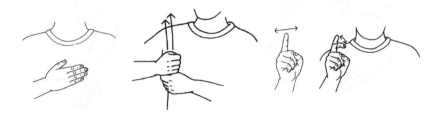

English: I want that skirt.
Sign: SKIRT — THAT (one) — WANT ME

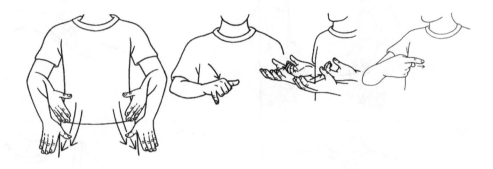

English: Where is my wallet?
Sign: MY WALLET — WHERE Q

English: If you wear a blouse, I'll wear a tie.
Sign: IF BLOUSE YOU WEAR — TIE ME WEAR

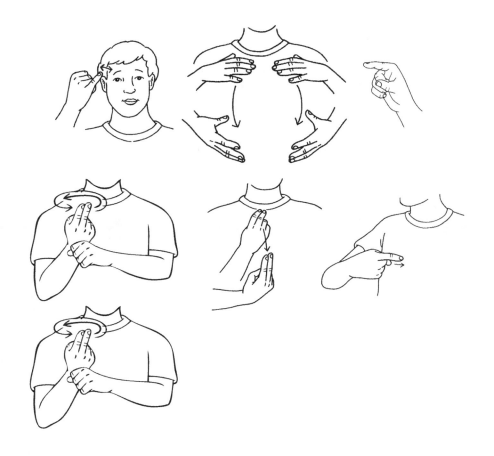

English: Her purse is nice.
Sign: HER PURSE —NICE

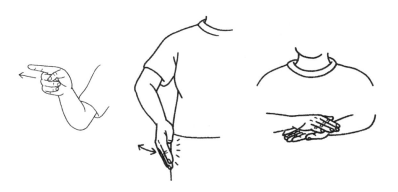

Summer suits

You can let everyone know your taste in summer wear with just a few bare-bones signs. Table 9-6 gives you the hottest signs for the coolest summer clothes.

TIP

To sign **sunglasses,** just put the sign for **sun** before **glasses.** For a **two-piece swimsuit** for women, you sign **bra** and **panties;** for a **one-piece swimsuit,** you sign **one piece.** You fingerspell **men's swimming trunks,** or you can sign **shorts.** But if you're talking Speedos, sign it like **panties.**

TABLE 9-6   ## Summer Sizzlers

English	Sign	English	Sign
SHORTS		SUNDRESS	
SUNGLASSES		SANDALS	

Now that you have the summer basics, try these sentences:

English: Where did you buy those sunglasses?
Sign: SUNGLASSES — BUY YOU — WHERE Q

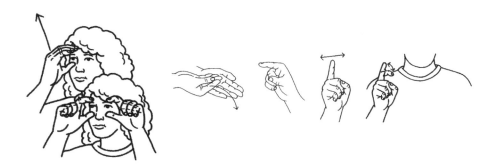

English: These shorts are old.
Sign: SHORTS (point) — OLD

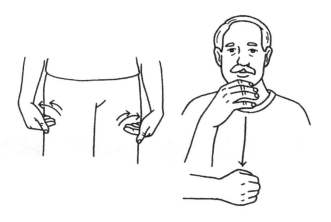

English: When will the T-shirt shop open?
Sign: T-SHIRT SHOP — OPEN — WHEN Q

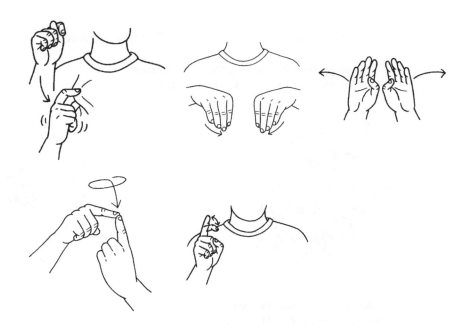

Clothing by color

Adding color to the canvas only brightens your repertoire of Sign. Time to bring it all home. This section gives you a start with your basic colors. Use the signs in Table 9-7 to mix and match your way throughout the year.

TABLE 9-7   **Common Colors**

English	Sign	English	Sign
BLACK		BLUE	

English	Sign	English	Sign
BROWN		GREEN	
ORANGE		PINK	
PURPLE		RED	
WHITE		YELLOW	

Following are some sentences that let you practice your newfound coloring skills:

English: Her dress is blue and white.
Sign: HER DRESS — BLUE WHITE

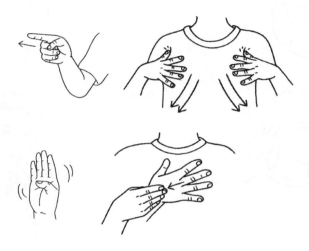

English: His tie is green.
Sign: HIS TIE — GREEN

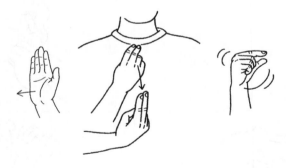

English: He wore a yellow cotton shirt.
Sign: FINISH — HE WEAR SHIRT — YELLOW COTTON

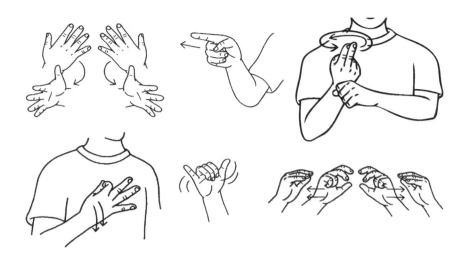

English: Her purse was black leather.
Sign: FINISH — HER PURSE — BLACK LEATHER

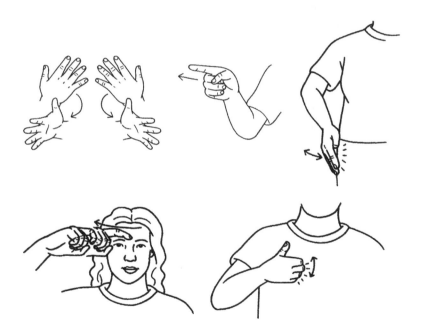

Signin' the Sign

 Aurora and David are going shopping. The stores have many sales, and they're looking for the best deals. Follow along as they move through the aisles.

Aurora: That blue dress is pretty.
Sign: BLUE DRESS — PRETTY

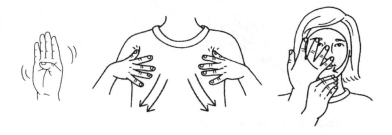

David: Those brown shoes are big.
Sign: BROWN SHOES — BIG

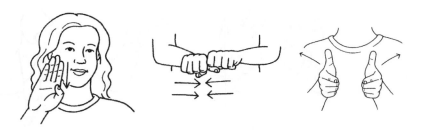

Aurora: Do you like the black slacks?
Sign: BLACK SLACKS — YOU LIKE Q

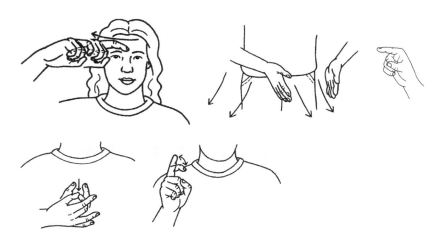

David: I like the leather pants.
Sign: LEATHER PANTS — LIKE ME

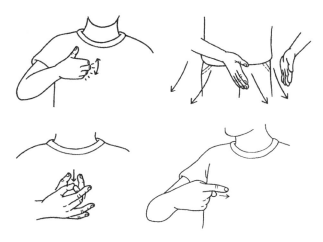

All about Money

Now comes the not-so-fun part — paying for all your new items. But because you have to fork over the money, the signs in Table 9-8 cover the variety of ways to pay for those purchases.

TIP

When signing **ATM/debit card** or **credit card,** outline a card shape after making the signs in Table 9-8.

TABLE 9-8 ## Payment Options

English	Sign	English	Sign
ATM/DEBIT CARD		CASH	
CHARGE		CHECK	
CREDIT CARD		OWE	

Table 9-9 covers other money-related words.

TABLE 9-9   **Financial Words**

English	Sign	English	Sign
BANK		BILLS/DOLLARS	
CENTS		CHANGE	
MONEY		PAY	

Here are some financial-transaction sentences for you to practice money matters:

English: I'll pay with my credit card.
Sign: CREDIT (outline card) — PAY WILL ME

English: She wrote a $50 check.
Sign: FINISH — CHECK 5-0 DOLLARS — WRITE HER

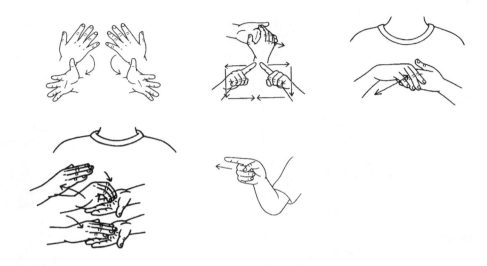

English: The bank gave me an ATM card.
Sign: A–T–M (outline card) — B–A–N–K — GIVE ME

TIP

You can sign **credit card** two different ways. The old way is shown in Table 9-8. The new way: Outline a card shape and then show the motion of swiping it through a machine.

Signin' the Sign

Robert and Krista are going clothes shopping. They like to save money, so they're doing some comparison shopping.

Robert: I'm buying new clothes.
Sign: NEW CLOTHES — BUY ME

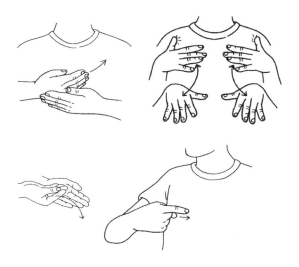

Krista: I don't have a lot of money.
Sign: A LOT MONEY — HAVE ME — NOT

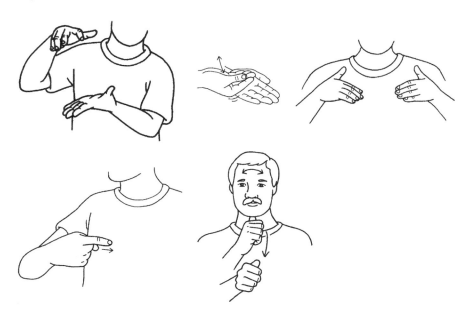

Robert: Buy a couple of blouses on sale.
Sign: TWO BLOUSES — SALE — BUY

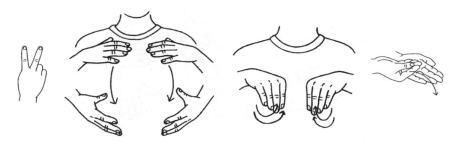

Krista: If I buy blouses, I'll need pants.
Sign: IF BLOUSES BUY — PANTS NEED ME

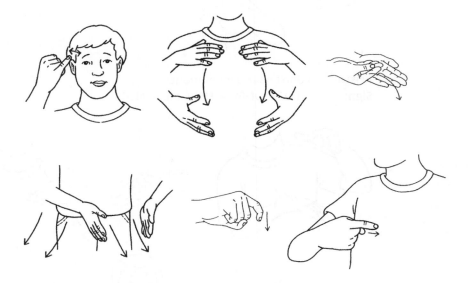

Robert: Use your credit card.
Sign: CREDIT (outline card) — YOURS USE

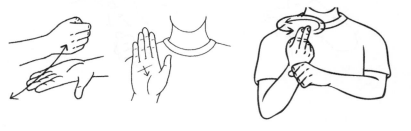

Shopping Superlatives and Comparisons

In English, you sometimes form words that compare by adding endings, such as "er" or "est." For comparatives and superlatives in Sign, you use the root (base) word and then add a modifier. For example, you sign **greatest** simply as **great,** and you sign **happier** as **happy.** After you decide which base word you want to use, sign it and then add one of the words from Table 9-10 — whichever one is the most appropriate.

TIP

Comparing costs is a pretty common thing to do. Here's how to sign the better bargain. If you're at the store, you can always point to what you're referring to; that way you can avoid fingerspelling. To sign that you found the cheapest or most expensive item, simply sign **cheap** or **expensive** and then sign the word **top.** This is a good way to compare several prices. You can also sign **cheap** or **expensive** and then sign **better.**

TABLE 9-10   ## Super Words

English	Sign	English	Sign
GOOD		BETTER	
BEST		TOP	

(continued)

TABLE 9-10 *(continued)*

English	Sign		English	Sign
BOTTOM			BAD	
MINIMUM			MAXIMUM	
WORSE/ WORST				

English: The red shirt is better than the green one.
Sign: RED SHIRT — GREEN SHIRT — RED BETTER

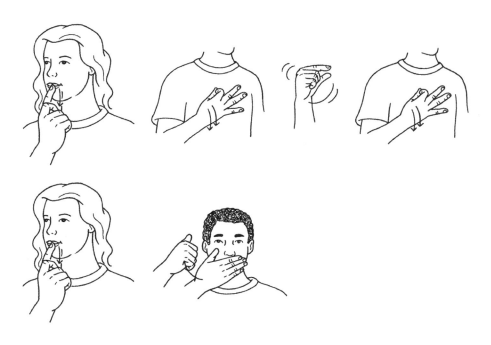

English: His coat is the warmest.
Sign: HIS COAT — WARM — TOP

English: Your shoes are the ugliest.
Sign: YOUR SHOES — UGLY — WORST

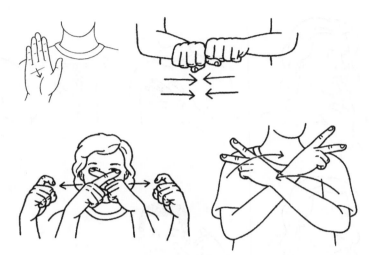

Chapter 10

The Signer About Town

Going out on the town, you see Deaf people signing at every turn. Because you're reading this book and discovering ways to communicate in American Sign Language, stopping to chat with them is no longer difficult.

The signs in this chapter give you an edge on conversing with other signers about the world of culture and entertainment. After you familiarize yourself with this chapter, you can discuss movies, plays, the theater, and even exhibits in a museum. You will also view signs to communicate your social status.

Making Plans

Getting together with friends has never been so easy. The signs in Table 10-1 help get you on your way.

TIP

Some timely tips to pencil in: **Appointment** and **reservation** are the same sign, so if you can sign one, you've got the other. The sign for **schedule** looks like the grid on a calendar page. You sign **socialize** with one thumb circling the other. **Write down** and **record** share the same sign. And the sign for **canceling an appointment or date** is exactly what you might expect — you make an **X** on your passive hand.

TABLE 10-1   **Planning Signs**

English	Sign	English	Sign
APPOINTMENT/ RESERVATION		CALENDAR	
CANCEL		SCHEDULE	
EVENT		WRITE DOWN	
SOCIALIZE		DELAY	

The following sentences are sure to help you make or break plans:

English: Write it down on your calendar.
Sign: YOUR CALENDAR — WRITE DOWN

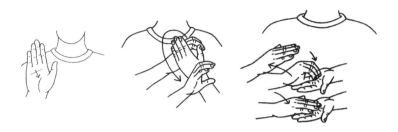

English: What is your schedule for tomorrow?
Sign: TOMORROW — YOUR SCHEDULE — WHAT Q

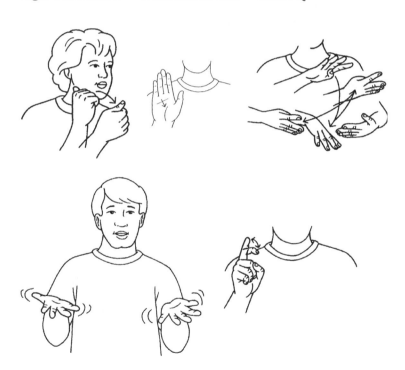

English: The event was cancelled.
Sign: FINISH — EVENT — CANCEL

You sign **finish** to show that the sentence is in past tense (see Chapter 2 for a discussion of tenses).

When you're giving the time or you need to sign what time something occurs, you touch your wrist where you normally wear your watch and then sign the number. For example, if you want to tell someone that it's 2 o'clock, touch your wrist and then sign the number **2.** To distinguish between a.m. and p.m., you sign **morning, afternoon,** or **night** after the number. This rule has two exceptions: For **midnight,** you don't touch your wrist; you simply sign the number **12** straight down. And for **noon,** you sign **12 noon** straight up.

Check out the signs for numbers in Chapter 4. You can then make a date for a specific day and time with the cute Deaf guy or girl you just met.

Going to the movies

You can sit around the house and watch a good TV program with your Deaf friends if your TV has closed-captioning (CC), which displays the text on the screen. If the captioning doesn't come on, just give it a minute.

Open-captioning (OC) is different. This captioning is the subtitles you usually see on foreign films, either at home on a DVD or out in the theater. In case you were wondering, yes, Deaf people do attend movies. Many Deaf people go to the movies to see the latest flicks and then go to dinner afterward. Some theaters have an OC night for newly released movies. This is a good place to meet Deaf people. Call your local theater to see whether it has a captioning night for the Deaf.

Some theaters don't have OC but do have *rear window* captioning. This involves a device that plugs into the seat's cup holder and extends in front of you, near eye level, displaying the movie's captions. You can also sometimes find *assistive listening devices* as well.

To sign **open-captioning,** simply fingerspell O–C.

Communicating during a movie is common among signers. They converse about everything — the movie's plot, an actor, or even the lack of salt on the popcorn! Table 10-2 presents some signs to help you enjoy the show.

TABLE 10-2   ## Movie and TV Terms

English	Sign	English	Sign
ACTING/ DRAMA/ STAR		CLOSED-CAPTIONED	
MATINEE		MOVIE	
SOLD OUT		TICKET	

Are you feeling a bit like Bond, James Bond, or are you more in the mood for bonding in a romantic way? Table 10-3 shows you signs that indicate various types of movies.

TABLE 10-3   ## Movie Genres

English	Sign	English	Sign
ACTION		COMEDY/ FUNNY	
MYSTERY		ROMANCE	
FANTASY		SCARY	

English: The movie sold out.
Sign: MOVIE — SOLD OUT

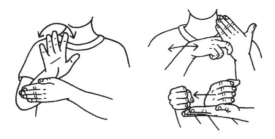

English: If the movie is open-captioned, I'll go.
Sign: IF MOVIE O-C — ME GO

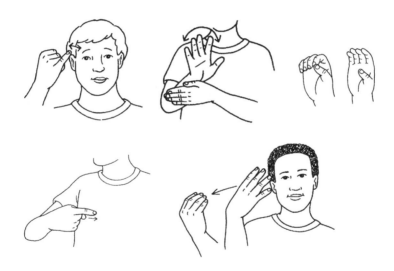

English: The matinee was a comedy.
Sign: AFTERNOON MOVIE — FUNNY

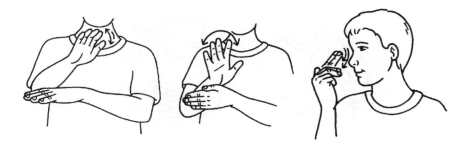

English: We went to see the new mystery.
Sign: FINISH — NEW MYSTERY — SEE US

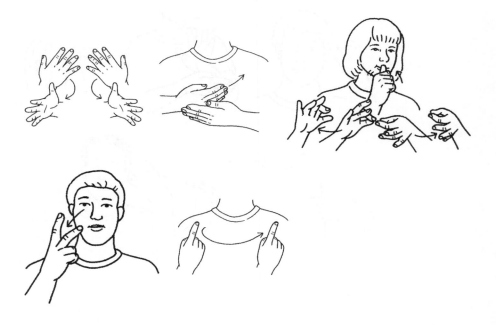

English: There's captioning Saturday at the movie.
Sign: SATURDAY MOVIE — O-C

Going to the theater

Attending plays is always a great way to improve your signing skills, especially if the actors also sign. Many plays provide an interpreter so that Deaf people can attend and enjoy the play along with hearing folks.

Table 10-4 shows you a few of the more well-known theatrical terms that you may want to know.

TABLE 10-4   **Theatrical Terms**

English	Sign	English	Sign
INTERMISSION		LIGHTS	
THEATER		STAGE	

TIP

You sign **light** with a double **flick,** using your index finger and thumb under your chin and then mimicking the action of screwing in or taking out a light bulb. You can also sign **light** and mimic shining a spotlight or a flashlight.

The sign for **stage** doesn't allow your passive hand to move — only the active one outward.

English: When the lights go out, stop talking.
Sign: LIGHTS OUT — TALKING STOP

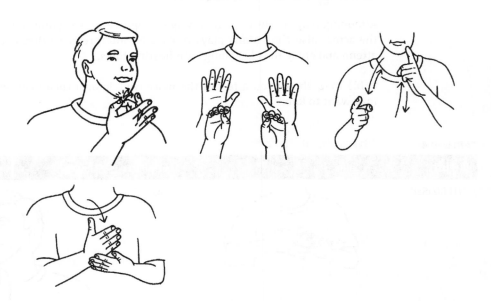

English: During intermission, I'm leaving.
Sign: DURING INTERMISSION — LEAVE ME

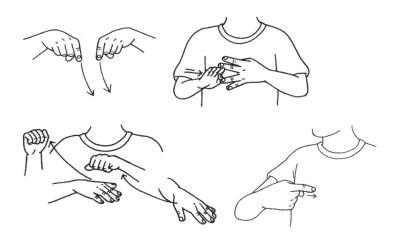

Going to the museum

Visiting a museum is quite an experience and one that many Deaf people can appreciate as easily as those in the hearing world. You don't have to be able to hear to enjoy all the wonderful things that are included in museums. However, being able to discuss what you see is nice.

Use the signs in Table 10-5 when you go back in time for a few hours.

TABLE 10-5 **Museums and Museum Displays**

English	Sign	English	Sign
ART		DISPLAY/ EXHIBIT/ SHOW	
HISTORY		MUSEUM	

(continued)

TABLE 10-5 *(continued)*

English	Sign	English	Sign
PHOTOGRAPHY		SCULPTURE	
TIME/ERA		BROCHURE	

TIP

You sign **museum** like "house," only you use the manual **M** on both hands. You sign time periods by signing the manual **T** in a circular motion with your active hand on your passive hand. This means **time period** or **era.**

TIP

You sign **photography** by mimicking taking a picture. Make sure that you give it a double click because a single click means "to take a picture."

English: The museum is open.
Sign: MUSEUM — OPEN

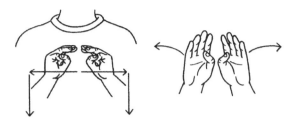

English: We saw the photography exhibit.
Sign: FINISH — PHOTOGRAPHY EXHIBIT SEE

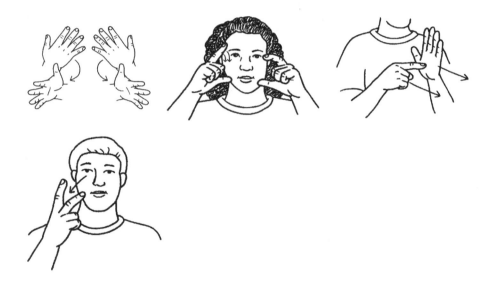

Selecting Your Social Station

Going out with the gang is a good time for those who like the night life. Deaf people enjoy their social bonds and can paint the town red with the best of them. Often, people go as singles, and other times, it's couple's night out. The signs in Table 10-6 will help you when you're planning that night out with your friends. At night, signs just seem to flow.

TABLE 10-6 **Social Station Signs**

English	Sign		English	Sign
MARRIED			SINGLE	
DIVORCED			BACHELOR/ BACHELORETTE	
DATE			FIANCÉ / FIANCÉE	

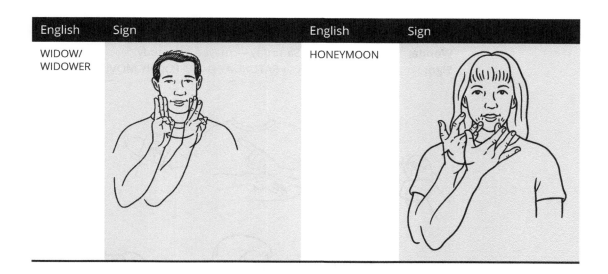

English	Sign	English	Sign
WIDOW/ WIDOWER		HONEYMOON	

Signin' the Sign

Denni and Wanda want to go to the movies, so they decide to schedule a time that works for both of them.

Denni: Want to go to a movie?
Sign: MOVIE — GO WANT Q

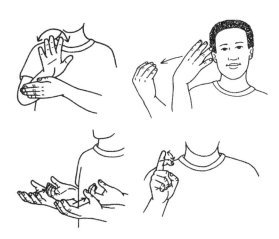

Wanda: Yes, I can go next Saturday — maybe a comedy.
Sign: YES — NEXT WEEK — SATURDAY — GO FUNNY MOVIE — MAYBE

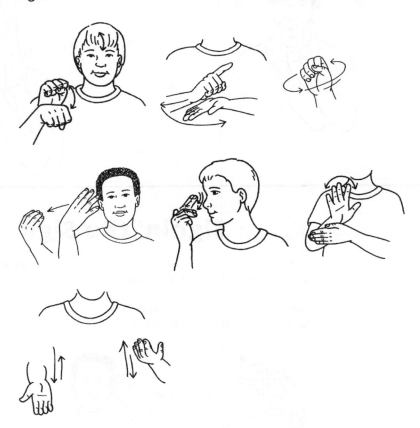

Denni: I'll write it down on my schedule.
Sign: SCHEDULE — WRITE DOWN — ME WILL

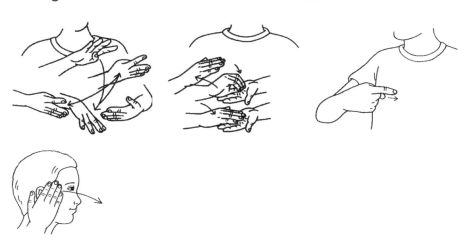

Wanda: I'll write it down, too.
Sign: WRITE DOWN — TOO — ME WILL

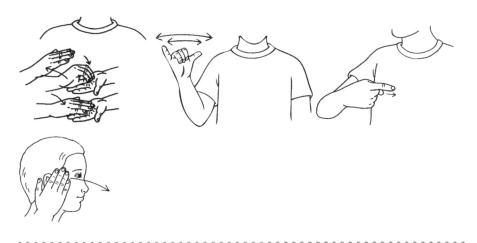

Chapter 11

Takin' Care of Business

M any more Deaf people work in office jobs than ever before, so there's never been a better time to know some signs for around the office. The signs in this chapter can help you show Deaf visitors around the office or communicate with a Deaf colleague at your workplace.

Occupying Yourself with Occupations

The average American worker changes occupations many times in the course of a career. Table 11-1 gives you signs for some job position terms.

TABLE 11-1   **Work Words**

English	Sign	English	Sign
ASSISTANT		BOSS	
WORKER/ EMPLOYEE		DIRECTOR/ MANAGER	
SECRETARY		SUPERVISOR	

Here are some sentences that will surely come in handy at the office:

English: When is payday?
Sign: PAYDAY — WHEN Q

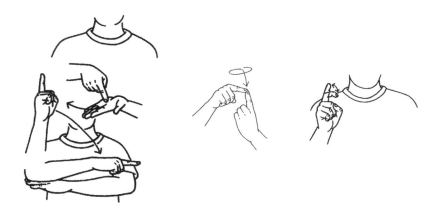

English: She was terminated by Human Resources.
Sign: H-R TERMINATE HER

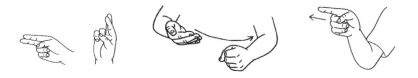

Most people refer to Human Resources as "HR," so you sign this term by finger-spelling H-R.

REMEMBER

English: The boss has my time sheet.
Sign: TIME SHEET MINE — BOSS HAVE

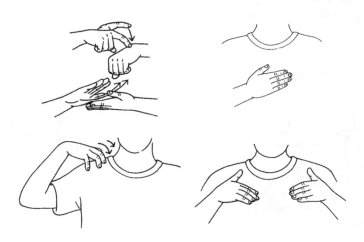

Signin' the Sign

Maria is a new office employee. Her trainer is George. She wants to do well at her new job and asks George questions so she will know what to do in her new work environment.

Maria: Is that the manager?
Sign: MANAGER — HIM (point) Q

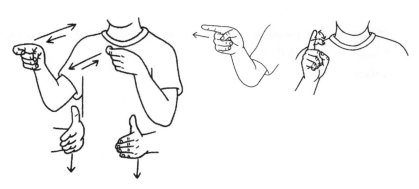

George: No, he is the assistant manager.
Sign: NO — ASSISTANT MANAGER — HIM

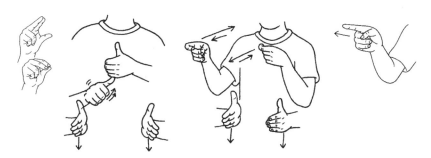

Maria: Where is the boss?
Sign: BOSS — WHERE Q

George: In a meeting.
Sign: MEETING

Maria: Who is my supervisor?
Sign: MY — SUPERVISOR — WHO Q

George: Dee, she is a good boss.
Sign: D-E-E — GOOD BOSS — TRUE (affirmation)

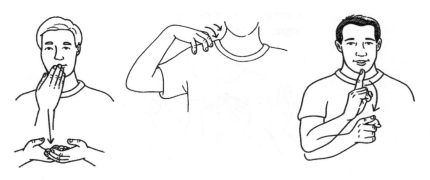

Sorting Office Supplies

Moving around the cubicle, you have many things to sign. Try the signs in Table 11-2 and you'll be the boss.

TIP

You may find the sign for **clock** to be a bit tricky, but it's really pretty simple. Touch your wrist where you wear your watch and then make both hands into manual L handshapes that are bent at the knuckle toward the wall or wherever the clock is located.

TABLE 11-2   ## Office Equipment

English	Sign	English	Sign
CLOCK		OFFICE	
PAPER		COPY MACHINE	

(continued)

TABLE 11-2 *(continued)*

English	Sign	English	Sign
PAPER CLIP		DESK/TABLE	
PENCIL		EQUIPMENT	
PHONE		LAPTOP	
STAPLER			

The office is a great place to work these signs. The following sentences can give you a hand with some office items. And because office equipment doesn't always work, signs exist for that, too.

English: The copy machine is broken.
Sign: COPY MACHINE — BROKE

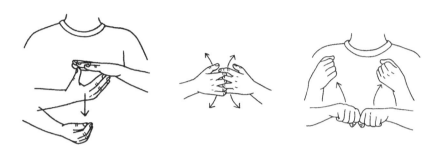

REMEMBER

Sign **broke** or **broken** like you're breaking a stick with both hands in the manual S handshape.

English: My computer is frozen.
Sign: MY COMPUTER — FROZE

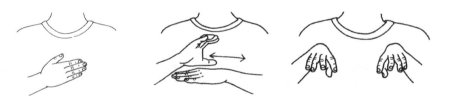

REMEMBER

Sign **froze** or **frozen** like the word **freeze** (see Chapter 5).

English: Where is the stapler?
Sign: STAPLER — WHERE — Q

English: Do we have enough paper?
Sign: PAPER — ENOUGH — HAVE — Q

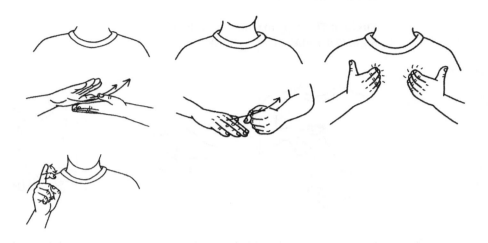

Getting to Work

The workaday world is full of tasks, from stocking shelves to attending meetings. The signs in Table 11-3 make work a little more fun; you can carry on a private conversation with another signer during a boring meeting.

TABLE 11-3   Business Terms

English	Sign	English	Sign
BUSINESS		CLOSED DOWN (as in computer screen)	

English	Sign	English	Sign
DISCUSS		MEETING/CONFERENCE	
PROMOTION		TRADING (stocks)	
WORK			

Put these work-related signs into action in the following sentences:

English: Are you going to the conference?
Sign: CONFERENCE — GO —YOU — Q

English: The managers meeting is upstairs.
Sign: MANAGERS MEETING — UPSTAIRS

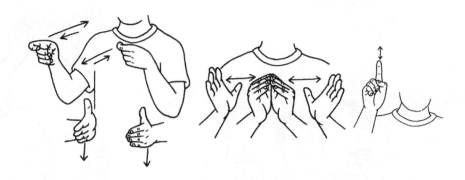

English: If you trade stocks, I will, too.
Sign: IF TRADE — YOU — ME — SAME

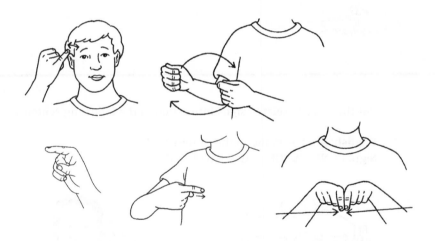

English: Where do you work?
Sign: WORK—YOU—WHERE — Q

English: The business is closed.
Sign: BUSINESS CLOSED

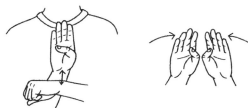

Chapter 12

Recreation and the Great Outdoors

You can relax in many ways. This chapter covers a few of the more active pastimes. We provide signs for sports, recreations, and hobbies in this chapter. And because you probably don't want to have a picnic in the rain, this chapter also deals with signs for the weather.

Exercising Your Right to Recreate

All work and no play makes Jack a dull boy — or so the saying goes. The point is that everyone loves to get out and play once in a while, whether on a team or individually. This section gives signs for various team sports first, and then, for those of you who are more independent, signs for solo sports. Have fun!

Getting into the competitive spirit

The majority of sports signs look like what they represent. For example, the signs for **tennis** and **baseball** mimic the swing of a racket and bat, respectively. Don't you just love it when signing is this easy? Check out Table 12-1 for more team sports signs.

TABLE 12-1 ## Competitive Team Sports

English	Sign	English	Sign
BASEBALL		BASKETBALL	
BOXING		FOOTBALL	
HOCKEY		SOCCER	
WRESTLING		TENNIS	

Signing **ball** is easy: Mimic putting both hands on a ball; do it with a double motion. You can make the ball as small or as big as you want.

You sign wrestling and football the same way: Lock your fingers together but don't bend them. If you do this with a double motion, that's **football**. If you lock your fingers once and go side to side, that's **wrestling.**

Box and **boxing** are the same sign. Put your fists up like you're in a boxing stance. No two people hold up their fists the same way, so the sign varies from person to person.

Table 12-2 gives you signs for competitive terms. Some of these signs are a bit tricky, so allow us to give you some explanation.

REMEMBER

You sign **match, game,** and **challenge** the same way, except the nouns **game** and **match** get a double motion while the verb **challenge** gets a single motion.

If you want to sign **versus,** use the same sign as the one for challenge.

REMEMBER

You sign **compete, sports,** and **race** the same way. Make the manual **A** handshape with both hands, put your palms together, and then alternate them back and forth. If you want to show fierce competition, grit your teeth and alternate your hands rapidly.

Signing **referee** or **umpire** is as simple as putting your index and middle fingertips on your lips, like blowing a whistle (and don't forget that double motion). You'll probably see many signs for these two words, but this sign seems to be pretty common.

TIP

Here's a helping tip: You sign **score** just like **count.** You may see some Deaf people sign one team's score on one hand and the other team's score on the other hand.

To sign **tournament,** start with both hands in the same handshape — index and middle fingers bent, palms facing the addressee, with your dominant hand higher than your passive hand. Now, alternate your hands up and down like making a bracket for a round-robin tournament.

Lose and **lost** are the same sign. Make the manual **V** handshape with your dominant hand and allow it to hit your passive palm and bounce up again.

TABLE 12-2 **Competitive Terms**

English	Sign	English	Sign
MATCH/GAME		CHAMPION/ CHAMPIONSHIP	
RACE/COMPETE/ SPORTS		REFEREE/ UMPIRE	
SCORE		TEAM	
TOURNAMENT		LOSE/LOST	

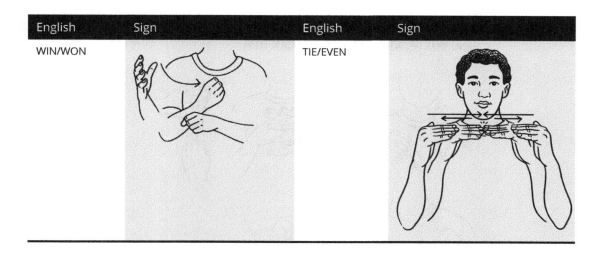

WIN/WON

TIE/EVEN

Here's how to put these signs into sentences:

English: The soccer game was good.
Sign: SOCCER GAME — GOOD

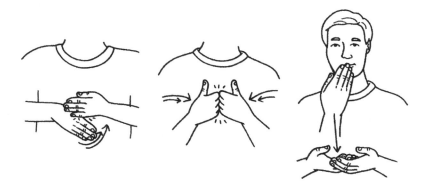

English: He can box and wrestle.
Sign: BOX — WRESTLE — BOTH CAN HIM

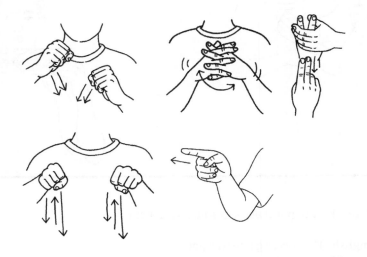

English: If you play soccer, you can't play basketball.
Sign: IF SOCCER PLAY YOU — BASKETBALL PLAY YOU — CAN'T

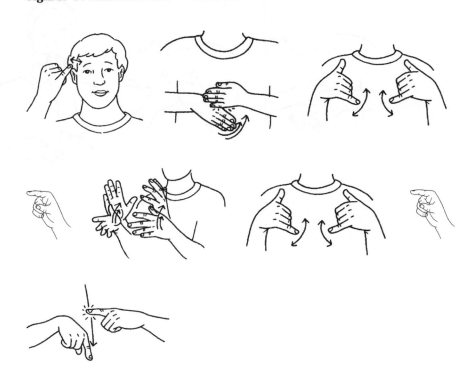

English: Our team won the race.
Sign: OUR TEAM — RACE — WON

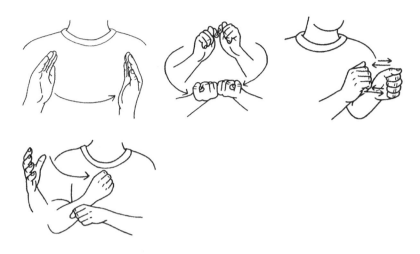

English: He's a football player.
Sign: FOOTBALL — PLAY HIM

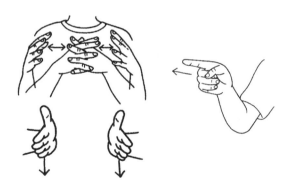

English: What's the score?
Sign: SCORE WHAT Q

English: Did we win or lose?
Sign: WIN — LOSE — US WHICH Q

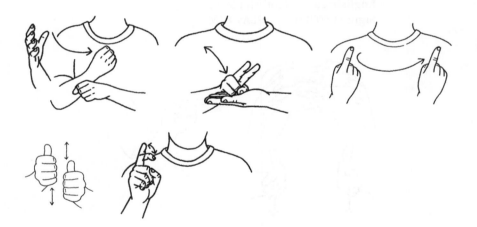

Setting out solo

You don't have to compete with a bunch of other people to be active and enjoy the great outdoors. Table 12-3 gives you the signs for sports that you can enjoy all by yourself if you want.

TABLE 12-3   Individual Sports

English	Sign	English	Sign
CYCLING		GOLF	
HIKING		JOGGING	
SWIMMING		RUNNING	
WALKING		ARCHERY	

When you sign **jog,** make fists, put them beside your body, and move them as though you're jogging, while alternating your arms.

TIP

Here are a couple of signs that aren't really about sports but are handy to know for outdoor activities:

PICNIC

CAMPING

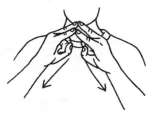

The following sentences show sports signs in action.

TIP

Glide your hands down the sides of your body after signing a sport to change from the sport to the player: golf to golfer, run to runner, and so on.

English: Mark is a good golfer.
Sign: M–A–R–K — GOOD GOLF (AGENT)

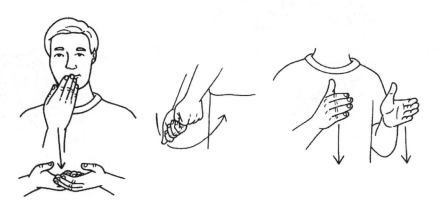

English: Do you like cycling?
Sign: CYCLING — YOU LIKE Q

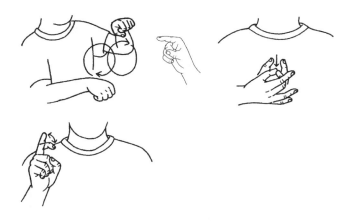

English: Let's go hiking.
Sign: HIKING — US GO

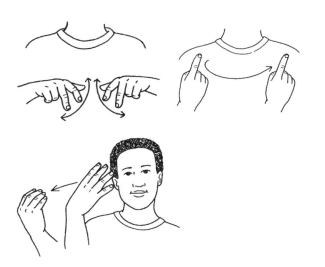

English: We're going on a picnic. Are you coming?
Sign: PICNIC GO US — COME YOU Q

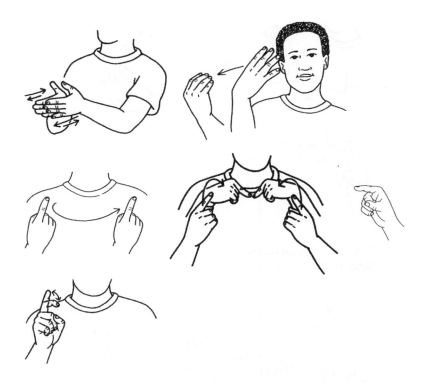

Playing Indoor Games

Not all games require a lot of physical activity. Nor do all of them have signs. For example, you fingerspell **cards, chess,** and **checkers.** You also fingerspell all board and card games. Mimic throwing dice for **gambling** and dealing cards for any **card game.** After you do this, fingerspell specifically what game you mean. Some indoor games do have signs, though, and you can find many of them in Table 12-4 — no cheating!

REMEMBER

If your Deaf friends have a local sign for a game, just use that sign instead.

TABLE 12-4   **Indoor Games**

English	Sign	English	Sign
BETTING		BOARD GAME	
DEAL CARDS		GAMBLING	
VIDEO GAMES		Phone Games	

English: Who wants to play poker?
Sign: P-O-K-E-R — PLAY — WANTS — WHO Q

English: Deal the cards.
Sign: DEAL CARDS

English: He likes playing chess.
Sign: C-H-E-S-S — HE LIKES

English: Do you gamble?
Sign: GAMBLE — YOU Q

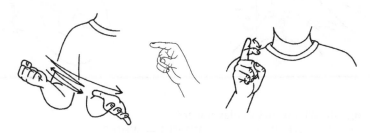

Having Fun with Hobbies

From collecting to surfing the web, hobbies keep you busy, entertained, and sometimes even educated. The signs in Table 12-5 show you how to tell people about your hobby and make it come alive!

TABLE 12-5　　**Hobbies**

English	Sign	English	Sign
COLLECTING		BROWSING THE INTERNET	
KNITTING		READING	
SEWING		STAMP COLLECTING	

TIP

You sign **browsing the Internet** by showing the sign for **Internet** and then signing **search.** To sign **stamp collecting,** sign **stamp** and then **collect** — like gathering a bunch of stamps into the palm of your hand.

English: I collect stamps.
Sign: STAMPS — COLLECT ME

English: Knitting is relaxing.
Sign: KNITTING — RELAXING

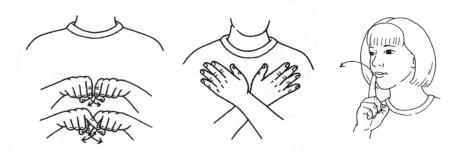

English: I like sewing.
Sign: SEWING — LIKE ME

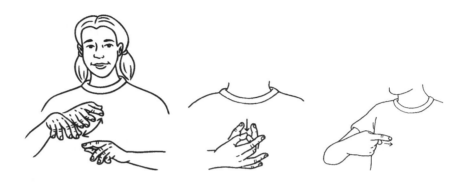

Seeing the Night Sky

Enjoying the serene beauty of the night sky is one of nature's most wonderful pleasures. Only one thing is better — having your new Deaf friends along to take in the view. Because American Sign Language is a visual language and the night sky is a visual phenomenon, it's fitting to see how these two awesome pleasures come together. The signs listed in Table 12-6 are fun to learn and fun to sign because there's movement involved — a shooting star, an eclipse of the moon, and a twinkling, star-filled sky are only a few examples.

TABLE 12-6   **Celestial Signs**

English	Sign	English	Sign
STAR		SHOOTING STAR	

(continued)

TABLE 12-6 *(continued)*

English	Sign	English	Sign
FULL MOON		CRESCENT MOON	
SKY		STAR-FILLED SKY	
ECLIPSE		HEAVENS	
SUN			

English: Did you see the shooting star?
Sign: FINISH — SHOOTING STAR — SEE— Q

English: The eclipse was red.
Sign: ECLIPSE — RED — TRUE (affirmation)

Getting the Weather Report

When isn't the weather a popular topic for discussion? Practice the basic weather signs in Table 12-7 and you'll be as right as rain. And because one should always be prepared, Table 12-8 provides signs for dealing with natural disasters.

TABLE 12-7   ## Weather Wise

English	Sign	English	Sign
CLOUDY		DARK	
THUNDER		LIGHTNING	
STORM		SUNNY	

English	Sign	English	Sign
WINDY		OUTSIDE	
WEATHER		RAIN	

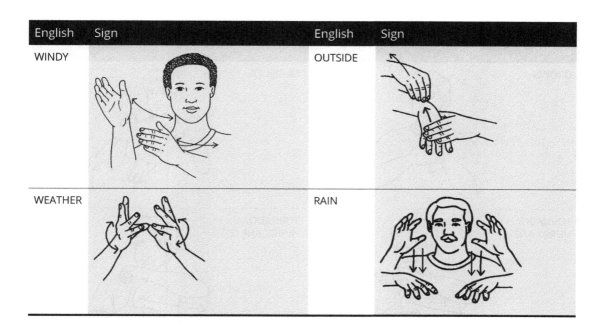

TABLE 12-8 ## Natural Disasters

English	Sign	English	Sign
EARTHQUAKE		TSUNAMI	
FLOOD		FIRE	

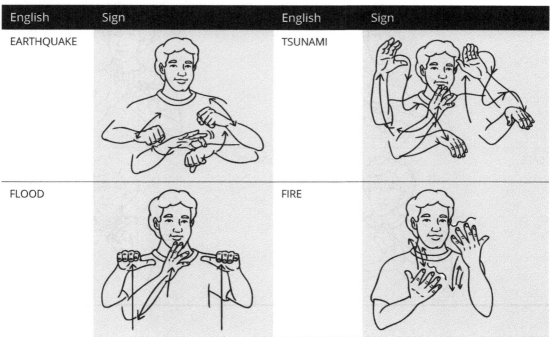

(continued)

TABLE 12-8 *(continued)*

English	Sign	English	Sign
DROWN		MUDSLIDE	
TORNADO/ HURRICANE (1)		TORNADO/ HURRICANE (2)	
WARNING		ALERT	
SAFE		ESCAPE	

Check out these weather signs and give them a whirl. Try replacing them with other weather signs — it'll be smooth sailing.

English: It is cloudy today.
Sign: TODAY — CLOUDY

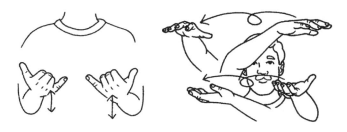

English: It's sunny outside.
Sign: OUTSIDE SUNNY

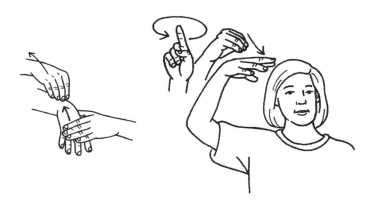

English: It's dark and windy this evening.
Sign: NOW NIGHT — DARK WINDY

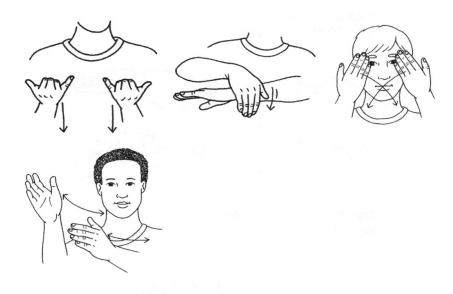

English: There is thunder and lightning outside.
Sign: OUTSIDE — THUNDER LIGHTNING

Asking Rhetorical Questions in ASL

What you know about rhetorical questions in English is not the same as rhetorical questions in ASL. In English, a rhetorical question is a question that does not require an answer. In ASL, a rhetorical question is asked and the person who asks the question gives the answer as well. A rhetorical question is a way of making a point by providing the information for the very question you ask.

TIP

Keep your eyebrows up when you ask the question — that action tells everyone that you don't expect an answer. And if you're on the receiving end of a rhetorical question, you'll recognize it because the signer will barely pause before answering his own question. His hands won't go down to give you a chance to put your hands up to respond.

REMEMBER

When you ask a rhetorical question, you use **who, what, why, where, when,** and **how** (which are covered in Chapter 6) to make the sentence rhetorical, but you don't add a question mark because you aren't really asking a question. You are setting up the question to answer it yourself.

English: Brent is on my team.
Sign: MY TEAM-- WHO — B-R-E-N-T

English: The tournament is in Pueblo.
Sign: TOURNAMENT WHERE — P-U-E-B-L-O

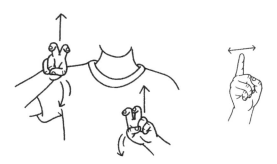

Signin' the Sign

 Jason and Jesse can't decide what they want to do tomorrow — it just depends on the weather.

Jesse: I want to golf tomorrow.
Sign: TOMORROW — GOLF — PLAY WANT ME

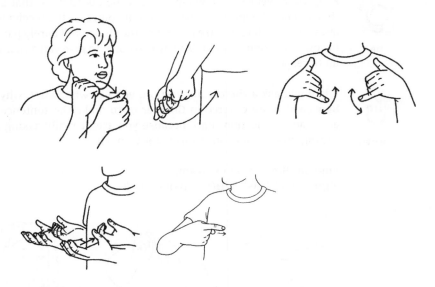

Jason: I'll go swimming tomorrow.
Sign: TOMORROW — SWIM ME

Jesse: If it rains, are you going swimming?
Sign: IF RAIN — YOU SWIMMING Q

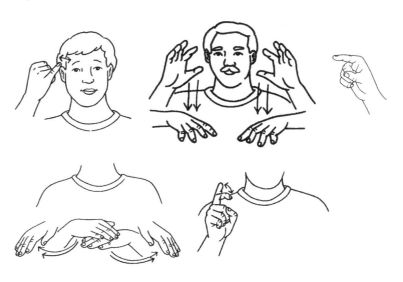

Jason: No, I'll stay home and read.
Sign: NO — HOME STAY — READ

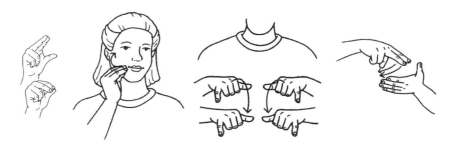

Jesse: If it rains, let's play cards.
Sign: IF RAIN — CARDS US

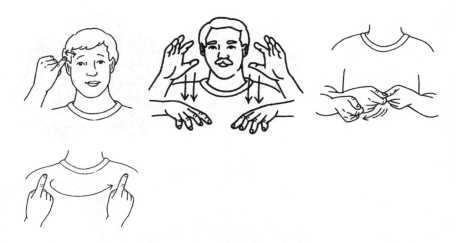

Chapter 13

Here's to Your Health

The medical field has many signs, and practicing them is fun. However, health and medicine are serious issues. Knowing the following medical signs doesn't automatically make you a medical interpreter, but that knowledge can go a long way in helping someone with an illness or emergency. In this chapter, we cover some of the main medical-related signs.

Going to the Doctor

Doctor visits ensure good health. In this section, we give you the signs to communicate successfully with medical personnel and tell them your symptoms. These signs are more helpful than an apple a day — try them and see.

Signaling medical personnel

The doctor is in! Table 13-1 shows the signs for various medical people.

TABLE 13-1   Medical Personnel

English	Sign	English	Sign
CHIROPRACTOR		DENTIST	
DOCTOR		NURSE	
SPECIALIST		SURGEON	

The following sentences are sure to come in handy.

English: Do you need a nurse?
Sign: NURSE — NEED Q

English: The doctor is in.
Sign: DOCTOR HERE

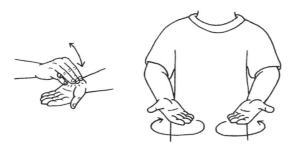

English: You need to see a chiropractor.
Sign: CHIROPRACTOR — NEED YOU

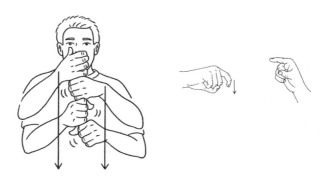

Figuring out how you feel

Knowing the signs for symptoms of an illness helps you figure out the best way to handle a medical problem. As with talking, signing is sometimes difficult when you don't feel well, but it's a necessary part of receiving help. The signs in Table 13-2 can take the sting out of communicating your problem.

TABLE 13-2   **Feelings/Symptoms**

English	Sign	English	Sign
COLD		CONSCIOUS	
DIZZY		EARACHE	
HEADACHE		NAUSEA	
UNCONSCIOUS		TEMPERATURE	

REMEMBER

You sign **conscious** the same way as **know** and **familiar** or **aware**.

You sign **knocked out** as K-O. With your dominant hand, start the K handshape at eye level, with the O handshape ending at the side of your mouth. Complete the sign with your eyes closed while bending your head to the side or in front.

Feeling healthy, wealthy, and wise is great, but allow us to talk about the word *feel*. Sign **feel** by running your middle finger up your stomach, your chest, and outward. If you put your thumb up after signing feel, it means **feel good**.

FEEL

Expressing medical terms

Medical words are simple in Sign; they usually look like what they mean. For example, you sign **blood pressure** by making a C handshape with your dominant hand and then placing it on your arm muscle. You then mimic working a pump bulb. You sign **sutures** and **stitches** by mimicking that you're putting a needle in and out of the stitched area. Check out Table 13-3 to see for yourself.

TABLE 13-3   **Medical Procedures**

English	Sign	English	Sign
BANDAGE		BLOOD PRESSURE	
DRAW BLOOD		INJECTION	

(continued)

TABLE 13-3 *(continued)*

English	Sign	English	Sign
SURGERY		SUTURE/STITCH	
TEST		LIE DOWN	

Some signs are similar in appearance. After you adjust to visually reading American Sign Language, you'll be comfortable in determining a sentence's context.

Try the following sentences for practice.

English: I need to check your blood pressure.
Sign: YOUR — BLOOD PRESSURE — CHECK — ME — MUST

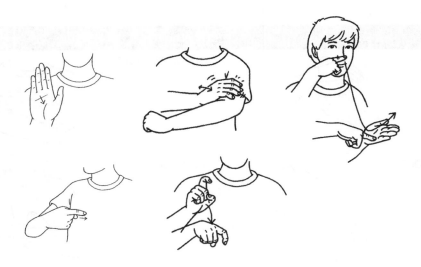

In ASL, you sign **I** and **me** the same way. Just point to yourself with your index finger. If you want a quick refresher, check out Chapter 6.

English: He needs an injection.
Sign: INJECTION — NEED — HIM

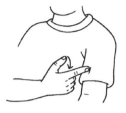

English: How do I get blood drawn?
Sign: ME — BLOOD DRAWN — HOW Q

You fingerspell some medical terms, especially those that are abbreviations anyway. For example, you use the manual alphabet to sign **CPR, ER, OR, MRI, ICU, IV,** and **X-ray,** as well as the names of medications.

Describing Ailments and Treatments

The ailments in Table 13-4 are signs that many ASL users run into — that explains the bruises! Try these signs anyway.

TABLE 13-4   **Ailments**

English	Sign	English	Sign
BREATHING PROBLEM (ASTHMA)		BRUISE	
COUGH		BROKEN BONE	
INFECTION		PAIN/HURT	
SICK/DISEASE		SORE THROAT	

The signs in Table 13-5 are the perfect relief. Practice them and you'll feel a whole lot better!

TABLE 13-5   ## Remedies

English	Sign	English	Sign
BED REST/ REST		CAST	
CRUTCHES		PRESCRIPTION	
WHEELCHAIR		MEDICINE	

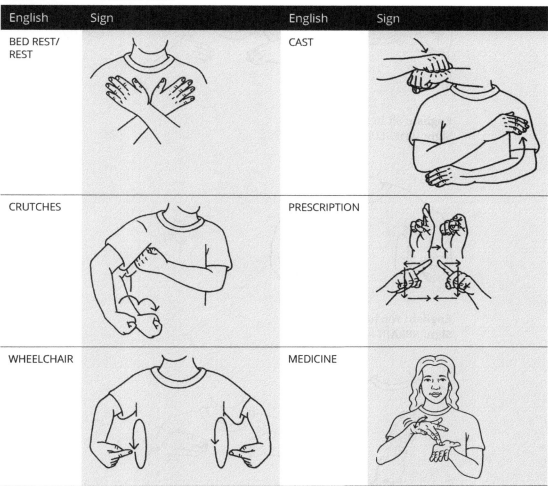

You sign **cast** by making the manual C handshape and placing it on your passive arm in a double sliding motion. If the cast is on a leg, point to the area. If it's a body cast, fingerspell B-O-D-Y C-A-S-T, or else you'll be pointing all day.

You sign **prescription** with the manual letters R-X and then a square with both index fingers starting at the top and meeting at the bottom — it means "slip."

If you're feeling up to it, try the following sentences.

English: She has an infection.
Sign: INFECTION — HAS — HER

English: Sit in the wheelchair.
Sign: WHEELCHAIR — SIT

English: You have a sprain.
Sign: SPRAIN — HAVE — YOU

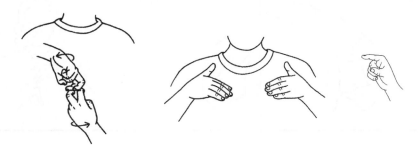

Pointing to Body Parts

If you're using ASL to describe ailments, it helps to be able to do more than point to the part that hurts, although in many cases, that's exactly how you sign differ-ent body parts. Tables 13-6, 13-7, and 13-8 illustrate the signs for body parts in three different groups. You sign most of the signs in these tables with a double motion; for example, for **ear,** tug twice on your earlobe.

TABLE 13-6   Parts of Your Head

English	Sign	English	Sign
EAR		EYE	
HEAD		JAW	
MOUTH		NOSE	
THROAT		TEETH	

TABLE 13-7

Bendy Places: Joints

English	Sign	English	Sign
ANKLE		ELBOW	
HIP		KNEE	
KNUCKLE		NECK	
WRIST			

TABLE 13-8 **Larger Body Parts**

English	Sign	English	Sign
ARM		BUTTOCKS	
CHEST		FEET	
HAND		LEG	

(continued)

TABLE 13-8 *(continued)*

English	Sign		English	Sign	
STOMACH			TORSO/TRUNK		

When you're not feeling that well, these sentences can help you get all the sympathy your hands can hold.

English: My throat is red.
Sign: MY THROAT — RED

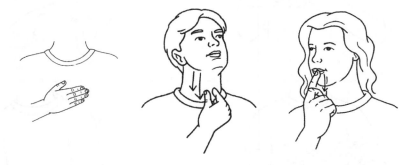

English: My neck is stiff.
Sign: MY NECK — STIFF

You sign **stiff** by using the same sign as **freeze.** With your hands in front of you, bend all your fingers slowly as if they're becoming frozen.

English: Can you cough?
Sign: COUGH — CAN YOU Q

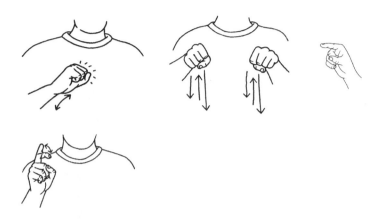

English: Her mouth is bleeding.
Sign: MOUTH BLEEDING — HER

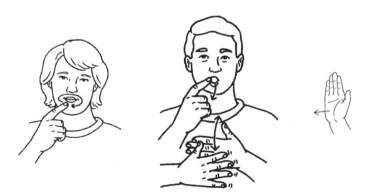

Handling Emergencies

Going to the hospital during an emergency is a scary thing. However, nothing is scary about these emergency-related signs (except having to use them). Table 13-9 may be your 9-1-1 when you need to help out in an emergency!

TABLE 13-9   **Emergency Room Talk**

English	Sign	English	Sign
ADMIT/ ENTER		AMBULANCE	
EMERGENCY		HEMORRHAGE/ BLEED	
HOSPITAL		DISCHARGE	

Hemorrhage is the same sign as **bleed**. To sign bleed, move your dominant hand up and down rapidly. The faster you do it, the heavier the bleeding.

TIP

Signin' the Sign

Lily and George are going to the hospital; he is ill and needs medical attention. Read on and see how the story unfolds:

Lily: You need to get to the hospital.
Sign: HOSPITAL — GO — MUST YOU

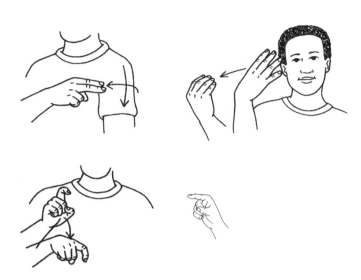

George: I'm dizzy and my stomach hurts.
Sign: DIZZY ME — STOMACH HURTS

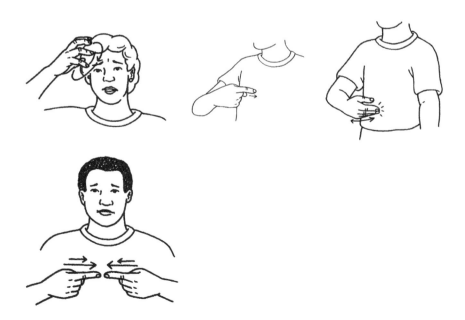

Lily: We'll go to the ER.

Sign: E-R — GO US — WILL

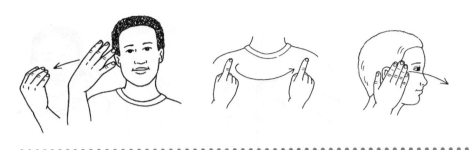

· ·

3

Looking at Life through Deaf Eyes

IN THIS PART . . .

Develop a sense of belonging and see the way of the Deaf, how they unite, who has united against them, what is acceptable to the Deaf community, and what is not.

Walk through history with and meet the Deaf who broke the barriers of oppression.

Learn how technology is allowing the Deaf to connect to the world in new ways.

Chapter 14

The Deaf Community and Deaf Etiquette

You probably picked up this book because you want to find out how to sign and communicate with Deaf friends, family members, or colleagues. But there's more to the Deaf community than just American Sign Language (ASL). In this chapter, you find out the history of Sign, the challenges that Deaf people have faced both past and present, and what it means to live in two cultures and speak two languages. This information can help you better understand just what it means to be Deaf, which, in turn, can help you better communicate with the Deaf people you know.

REMEMBER

Many people who can hear typically think Deaf people have a huge void in their lives because they can't hear. Nothing could be further from the truth. Even though Deaf people experience life a bit differently, they have a wonderful quality of life and enjoy the same things that hearing people do.

Digging into Sign's Past

The roots of ASL run fairly deep. Although early Greek writings refer to manual communication, no one knows whether those writings refer to just a few gestures or an actual alternative language using signs. Hippocrates studied deafness, and Socrates believed that it was a natural occurrence for Deaf people to communicate manually.

CULTURAL
WISDOM

Juan Pablo Benet (1579–1629) wrote the first book, published in 1620, on how to teach Deaf people. He incorporated gestures, fingerspelling, writing, and speech.

You can find sign languages in every country throughout the world. Some countries, such as Canada and the United States, have similar sign languages, and their spoken languages are also similar. However, this isn't always the case. ASL is unique among the world's sign languages because it has had many influences and has influenced many sign languages of the world. This section explains the history of sign language, how the Deaf view themselves, their history with interpreters, and how these two worlds come together.

Examining When and How ASL began

Many people believe that ASL was strongly influenced by the work of Thomas Hopkins Gallaudet and Laurent Clerc in the early 1800s at the American Asylum in Hartford, Connecticut (see the nearby sidebar, "The origins of Deaf education").

Another influence of ASL's origin goes back long before the arrival of Gallaudet and Clerc. In the 17th century, Deaf people were living in the United States. They lived in their own communities on Martha's Vineyard and made their livings as farmers and fishermen. Most of these inhabitants were descendants of people who'd moved to America from England. Two hundred years later, their descendants were still living there and attending the American School for the Deaf under Clerc and Gallaudet. Many believe that the signs brought to America by these educators and the signs used by the Martha's Vineyard population are largely responsible for today's ASL.

REMEMBER

ASL isn't related to English, although it borrows from English — as many spoken languages do. ASL has a word order that's different from English, and it has its own idioms, jokes, and poetry — all unrelated to English. People who support ASL believe that anything can be taught in ASL because it's a language guided by properties.

Sign is visually based. An object, such as a person, animal, or thing, needs to be understood by two parties before any information can be signed concerning the subject. Some people believe that this is the natural process for language. Many languages are based on this idea — it's the noun-verb rule. You need to name an object before you can discuss it.

Facing the Challenges of the Deaf Community

Through the years, Deaf people have had to face numerous challenges. In the past, they had little access to education and almost no opportunity for gainful employment. Although things have improved over time, Deaf people still face challenges. This section discusses challenges past and present and looks at how the Deaf community has made strides to overcome them.

Putting the past behind us

Sign language, like the Deaf people who use it, has had to fight for survival. Around the world, sign language — as well as those who communicate this way — has been viewed as lesser than languages of the hearing world. Many hearing people have dedicated themselves to changing the Deaf and their language.

For centuries, Deaf people had to undergo the treatment of being viewed as incomplete because of their absence of hearing. Some religious groups wanted to *save* Deaf people, while other groups wanted to *teach* them. Because of a lack of speech, Deaf people were viewed as deaf and dumb. This label, which Aristotle invented, has been attached to Deaf people since ancient Greece.

Deaf people have been associated with being demon-possessed because some of them can't speak. Because numerous biblical verses label Deaf people as dumb and/or mute, the Middle Ages — a dogmatic religious time — wasn't kind to them. Deaf individuals were hidden by family members, locked in asylums, or forced to try speaking, even though they couldn't hear themselves.

During World War II, Adolf Hitler's henchmen castrated Deaf men after they were locked up in concentration camps as part of various medical experiments.

Contemporary religious leaders have attempted to heal Deaf people of their "sickness" and accused them of lacking faith when miraculous hearing didn't happen.

Some people mock signing in front of Deaf people or tell them how sorry they are that they can't hear the birds singing or the phone ringing. Others are so rude as to talk about Deaf people right in front of them as though they aren't even there.

Many Deaf people and Deaf advocates have risen to challenge this oppression, and they seem to have been successful, because Deaf people are still signing to one another every day.

You've come a long way, baby

Although Deaf people are no longer viewed as being possessed by the devil, they still continue to face the challenges presented to them by a hearing world. Deaf people have fought for equal opportunities in education and employment and for cultural recognition, just to name a few things. Take a look at how the Deaf community has overcome modern obstacles.

The laws of the land

The Americans with Disabilities Act (ADA) has been a milestone, not only for Deaf people but for all Americans. Here's some basic information about the ADA. This isn't intended to be legal advice but general information. To find out more about the ADA, go on the Internet and search for "Americans with Disabilities."

>> **Title I: Employment:** If 15 employees are deaf or disabled, the workplace must be modified to be accessible. For example, teletypes (TTY; see Chapter 16), ramps, and/or railings could be installed.

>> **Title II: Public Services:** Programs, activities, and transportation can't discriminate against disabled people. Buses, taxis, and other public means of transportation need to accommodate the disabled population. Programs

such as job training, educational classes, and other assistance to gainful employment must also be provided.

>> **Title III: Public Accommodations:** All new construction of establishments such as hotels, grocery stores, retail stores, and restaurants are mandated to add physical assistance, such as ramps and railings.

>> **Title IV: Telecommunications:** Telecommunication agencies that provide phone services must provide a relay service for TTY users.

>> **Title V: Miscellaneous:** Prohibits any threats to disabled people or to persons assisting the disabled.

Getting classified as an "official" language

Although the Deaf population in the United States has had much progress through laws promoting civil equality and educational advancement of Deaf people, the road to total equality is still a long one. Not all states in America recognize ASL as an actual language.

The dispute over whether ASL is an actual language has been ongoing. Those who think that it should be considered a language often cite the following reasons:

>> It syntactically contains properties like other languages, such as nouns, verbs, and adjectives.

>> It maintains grammar rules that must be followed.

Presently, most states in the U.S. support this argument and recognize ASL as a foreign language. In addition, numerous colleges and universities offer credits for ASL as a foreign language.

On the other hand, many people don't buy the argument that ASL is a real language. Their argument goes like this:

>> All countries, including the United States, use their own indigenous sign language. Therefore, if you were from Spain and traveled to Peru, your Spanish sign language wouldn't be compatible with Peruvian sign language, even though the hearing communities from both countries could speak Spanish and understand each other.

>> At best, some countries, such as the United States, have had a profound impact educationally on other countries. Many foreign Deaf people come to the United States for schooling, and they take home many ASL signs.

Standardizing a sign language internationally has not happened with any one national sign language. However, a sign language system called International Sign Language (ISL), previously called *Gestuno*, is used at international Deaf events and conferences. It uses various signs from several national sign languages and was first used in the 1970s at the World Federation of the Deaf in Finland. To get more information about ISL, contact Gallaudet University.

Living and working as part of the silent minority

In a real sense, Deaf people living in the United States are a silent minority. Living in a world where one's language is known by few and understood by even fewer influences how Deaf people view themselves. (To categorize how Deaf people view themselves is too big a label to put on people who are individuals with various educational, economic, social, and deafness levels. Some people are more adaptable than others — in both the hearing and Deaf worlds.)

Being understood by few also influences Deaf people's feelings about how to exist as a people. This experience is often compared to living in a foreign country. Think about it: How would you feel if you were living in a foreign land where the language, customs, and culture weren't native to you? You'd probably go through each day with reluctance and uncertainty. You'd want to say what's appropriate, not something that would be viewed as ignorant. You'd feel frustrated when you wanted to state your opinion but couldn't make yourself understood. You'd feel isolated when everyone was laughing at a joke and you didn't understand the punch line. Deaf people often feel this way when they're surrounded by hearing people.

When speakers of a minority group come together, apart from the majority, they feel a certain sense of freedom to be able to speak — or sign — as fast as they want, and to converse, using idioms in their native language.

The Deaf as an Ethnic Group

Although Deaf people don't share a commonality of skin color, they share a common bond of culture. If culture is defined as shared knowledge, experience, language, beliefs, and customs, Deaf people are definitely an ethnic group.

This self-awareness of a Deaf ethnic group has only been in existence since the 20th century. Deaf pride has come from this identification. These people view themselves as whole people, not people with broken ears, as the label *hearing impaired* implies. When a person is culturally Deaf, he identifies and sometimes introduces himself as Deaf. To be a member of a Deaf community, the ability to communicate in ASL is a basic requirement.

Understanding Deaf culture

Just like any other culture, the Deaf community has its own customs, beliefs, and arts that are passed down from generation to generation. The culture of the Deaf community isn't arbitrary; it's a system of understandings and behaviors. This cultural group shares the characteristics of other cultural groups:

>> The members share the commonalities of language and similar obstacles of daily life.

>> The Deaf culture is based on a collective mind-set, not on an individual one. Many Deaf people feel a stronger tie to other Deaf people than to people who can hear.

>> As Deaf people feel a strong bond to one another, they have a strong sense of cooperation.

>> Deaf people come from all walks of life, from executives to construction workers, and as is true in English, those who are more educated than others are able to communicate more clearly by following the rules of their respective language.

>> As with all cultures, time modifies and alters some aspects of the culture. This happens because culture is both learned and shared among a given group of people.

Culture teaches members of a community how they, as a people, respond to other ethnic groups and the world around them.

Knowing who falls into the Deaf cultural community

You may be thinking that the question of who fits into the Deaf community is a silly one — Deaf people, obviously! But the Deaf community includes these people, too:

>> **Hearing people:** Those who can hear play important roles in the community of the Deaf as educators, ASL teachers, and interpreters for the Deaf. Many hearing people are also married to Deaf people or have Deaf children, making them part of the Deaf community.

>> **Children of Deaf Adults (CODAs):** We say "children" because of the acronym, but obviously the term simply means people who have Deaf parents.

Living as bilingual/bicultural people

To be successful members of society, Deaf people have to be able to live and communicate in both the Deaf and the hearing worlds. They have to be comfortable navigating between the two — in other words, they have to be bilingual and bicultural. Proving that Deaf people can live as a bilingual, bicultural people, more Deaf people are attending college and working in white-collar jobs, and more interpreter training programs, which have Deaf instructors, are being established. Read the following examples to see this dual culture in action.

>> Many Deaf people have felt the burden of not having the spiritual satisfaction that people desire because most churches don't have anyone who knows Sign to interpret and minister to a Deaf member of the congregation. Today, however, many Deaf people are going into the ministry and leading their own Deaf congregations. Many hearing ministries are also learning ASL.

The Los Angeles Church of Christ's evangelist, Ron Hammer, learned Sign from Deaf members of the church. He trained these members in leadership, and the interpreters began an interpreter-training program inside the church. Today, the Deaf membership of that church has increased dramatically to become one of the largest Deaf congregational regions in Los Angeles.

We should note that many Deaf people prefer to attend an all-Deaf church. The sermons and testimonials in these churches are in Sign, and interpreters aren't needed.

>> Because Deaf people and hearing people share common interests and topics of conversation, they can use these commonalities to communicate and become closer. When a Deaf person is with his Deaf friends, he may talk about Deaf schools, but he can just as easily converse with a colleague at work about schools in general.

Topics such as the weather, sports, food, and entertainment are all popular (and are all discussed in various chapters of this book) with Deaf people as well as the hearing. Even topics that at first seem unique to the Deaf community are really similar to topics that are discussed by hearing people. For instance, Deaf people often discuss the nuances of ASL and "play on signs." Hearing people do the same when they play on words, making jokes and puns. Deaf people often converse about schools for the Deaf, discussing which ones they attended and their similar experiences with dorm life and residential supervision. Hearing people also talk about where they went to school, what they majored in, what dorm life was like, and so on.

>> Politics is a topic of Deaf conversation, the same as with hearing people. Deaf people also try to make sense of political affairs as they, too, have family members who are in the military in these troubled times.

>> Deaf people also enjoy the company of significant others. Conversations about dates, marriage, disagreements, and making up are topics most people, Deaf and hearing, have in common. Problems and solutions in relationships cross all cultural and linguistic barriers.

CULTURAL WISDOM

Sign language is not the same around the world. All countries have their own sign language. Interestingly, when two Deaf people meet and are from different countries, they have a higher chance of understanding each other as compared to two hearing foreigners who meet. Deaf people are used to being misunderstood or not understood at all and have to make extra efforts to get their point across.

Being Sensitive to Being Deaf

Being sensitive to Deaf people is a part of Deaf etiquette that's really for the hearing. Deaf people already know what it means to be Deaf, but those who can hear probably never think about the day-to-day struggles that the Deaf have to overcome in this world.

Getting close to a Deaf person requires a little vulnerability on both sides. Many Deaf people are just as insecure about not being understood as you are, but most of them are patient and incredibly skilled at getting their point across to you. Like all people, the Deaf come from all walks of life. Deaf men and women have the same careers that hearing people do — they're doctors, lawyers, teachers, homemakers, construction workers, and so on.

Living together in a hearing world

TIP

Here are some tips and hints to keep in mind when interacting with Deaf people:

>> As your signing progresses, a Deaf person may ask if your parents are Deaf. This is a high compliment about your signing. It doesn't mean that you're fluent in ASL, but it does mean that your signing or facial expressions have characteristics of being influenced by someone who's a native signer.

>> When visiting Deaf people, don't assume that you can just walk into the house because they can't hear the doorbell. Deaf people have strobe lights that are connected to the doorbell and the phone.

>> If you're out having a meal with a Deaf person, don't feel obligated to order for the person unless you're asked, even if it's just to practice your Sign. Deaf people have been eating in restaurants longer than you've been friends, and they're accustomed to pointing to an item on the menu for the server.

>> As you learn more signs, do your best to sign when you're talking with your hearing friends and a Deaf person joins the conversation. Signing what you're saying may be difficult, but you'll be able to do it in time with practice, and doing so helps the Deaf person feel included if he or she knows what you're saying.

Getting the Deaf perspective

After reading this book, no doubt you see that knowing Sign is just one piece (albeit a large one) of the puzzle to understanding the Deaf community. To really get a grasp on Deaf etiquette and culture, you have to get involved with the Deaf community. One sure way to get involved is to take an introductory ASL course from a Deaf instructor. Although you can find some awesome Sign instructors who can hear, a Deaf Sign instructor can teach from the Deaf perspective and is most likely a native signer.

An introductory class gives you exposure to signs, interaction with others and, hopefully, an opportunity to learn from Deaf guest speakers. You also get an understanding of the many signing styles that different people possess. An instructor can guide you as to where Deaf activities are taking place, who Deaf community leaders may be, and issues concerning the local community. Consider this class to be a segue to the Deaf community.

Participating in the Deaf Community

We can say a lot about the subject of participation in the Deaf community. A good rule to follow is, "When in Rome, do as the Romans do." In other words, when you're with Deaf people, respect their customs; what you don't know, you can figure out by observation and through asking questions. Basically, just watch and learn. Some of the things you may notice include the following:

>> **A sense of unity:** Depending on the size of the Deaf community, Deaf people congregate at activities such as bowling leagues, Deaf clubs, Deaf plays, and fundraisers. In Los Angeles, the Deaf community is very large. Subgroups inside the community consist of Russians, Chinese, Italians, Hispanics, Jews, and many others. Each of these groups has its own respective traditions, customs, and celebrations. As a whole community, they come together for events such as the Lotus Festival, Deaf West Theater, and Deaf Awareness Month.

>> **ASL pride:** Deaf people speak of ASL quite often in conversations. You may attend plays and parties where ASL is the main topic. The Deaf community is very proud and protective of this language, so it's often a hot topic.

>> **Signing speed:** When you watch Deaf people in conversation and you can't understand anything that's signed, don't lose heart. Novice signers often don't understand Deaf nuances and abbreviations, and they often have a hard time keeping up. Stay with ASL; before you know it, you'll be signing like a pro.

WARNING

And, just so you know, few things are more volatile in the Deaf world than a hearing person who, having taken a semester or two of ASL classes, proceeds to lecture a Deaf person because he or she doesn't sign the way the teacher instructed.

Finding your place in the Deaf community

As you find yourself with phone numbers of Deaf friends and invitations to Deaf socials, you'll be well on your way to being a constant student of ASL. Like everyone who studies, learning new ways of signing ideas will be commonplace. The possibility of going to school to professionally hone your skill and take classes in Sign may be an endeavor you soon realize.

Many people have no deafness in their families and learn ASL and Deaf culture at a rudimentary level. Time takes care of the rest as it gives way to proficiency through practice.

Some people have Deaf siblings or Deaf parents and know ASL through this avenue and understand Deaf culture because of them. These people have had deafness in their lives from the beginning.

All people who enter the Deaf world face a certain dynamic. Think of the dynamic as a bull's eye (see Figure 14-1). At the center is the core Deaf community leaders; these are the movers and shakers of the Deaf world. The next ring is the Deaf community as a whole. The next ring are Children of Deaf Adults, or CODAs, who are hearing people who choose to become interpreters. Following them are interpreters who have no Deafness in their respective families. On the outer ring are those who provide services to the Deaf community members but still have the ability to sign. These are teachers of the Deaf and can hear — vocational rehabilitation counselors, teachers at Deaf schools, and professional workers who provide services for the Deaf.

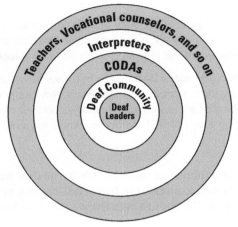

FIGURE 14-1:
Think of the layers of the Deaf community like a bull's eye.

© John Wiley & Sons, Inc.

Communicating with new Deaf friends for the first time

Joining the Deaf community is not something that anyone can just decide to do. Attending your first Deaf function with the Deaf person who invited you is appropriate. Attending a Deaf social without first receiving an invitation is never a good idea. As you arrive, your host, the one who invited you, will introduce you to his or her friends, explain how you know each other, and mention that you're learning ASL. Saying both your first and last name is customary, and a good rule of thumb is to let people know that you can hear and that you're learning Sign. They'll know this already by watching your lack of fluidity in the language; however, through this admittance and vulnerability, bonds of trust are made.

As you walk through the social, you'll notice Deaf people signing in fluent ASL, but when they see you approaching, they'll revert to signing in an English word order while using their voices. They do this to accommodate you. They already know that you can't keep up with their pace or fluency, and they change their modes of communication to make sure you can understand the conversation. This is called *code switching.* After you depart from the conversation, you'll notice that the Deaf people will go back to turning off their voices and will converse in proper ASL. Don't take this personally as an offense. The gesture of using more English by the Deaf folks for your benefit — code switching — is something that all hearing people experience when they attend Deaf socials for the first time.

Questions you shouldn't ask

WARNING

Never initiate a conversation about a Deaf person's hearing loss. Questioning someone about this implies that you don't view that person as whole, but broken, incomplete, or inferior. You'll find that the Deaf are comfortable talking about their hearing aids, batteries that need replaced, and ear molds, but it's best if you leave this subject to the individual who is Deaf. If you view a Deaf person with equality and respect, the hearing loss won't become a subject of any great importance. Often, as you become better friends, your questions will get answered in a passing conversation.

Just to satisfy your immediate curiosity, most Deaf people do not have a total hearing loss. They usually have what's called *residual hearing,* hearing that remains after deafness occurs, either at birth, after an illness or accident, or because of age. Deaf people have varying degrees of deafness; some are more profoundly deaf than others, so some Deaf people can speak clearly while others can't.

REMEMBER

In your time with the Deaf, make it a growing experience; you're encountering a people with a rich history, a proud people with a bond of community. You aren't the first person to want to know their language, and you won't be the last.

Interpreting for the Deaf Community

Interpreting for the Deaf community is very much a part of the Deaf experience.

Deaf people had started using family members as interpreters. Often the interpreter was usually the first female of the brood. Often when the Deaf parents needed an interpreter, they would rely on their children; professional, certified interpreters with a common standard was not established at this time.

The child with Deaf parents would interpret in a variety of situations. Deaf parents would depend on their children as laws requiring companies and agencies to provide ASL interpreters were also not yet established.

Deaf parents had to manage their business affairs through children who did their best but often did not have an adult mentality to understand adult things, planning funerals, medical appointments, car sales, apartment leases, and the like. Again, this was by no fault of the Deaf parents; professional interpreters were not what we know of today.

In was in 1964 at Ball State Teachers College that the Registry of Interpreters for the Deaf had its origins. This was the first meeting for using interpreters for Deaf people. However, Texas did have a society of interpreters that was established before the RID; the Texas Society of Interpreters for the Deaf was established in 1963.

Interpreters under the RID must adhere to a professional code of conduct, although this standard has changed throughout the years, confidentiality is still at the top of the list of tenets. Confidentiality is a matter of trust; this must be maintained at all times. Can you imagine a stranger knowing your personal information and telling other people? Think of having a medical appointment and the information gets back to your family; this must not happen. Although confidentiality is not the only tenet, it is the base to a professional relationship. If you cannot be trusted, you will find yourself without work.

Deaf etiquette is shown by Deaf having the right to ask if an interpreter is certified. Requesting a male or female interpreter is also appropriate. For a Deaf person to request a certain interpreter or not want a certain interpreter is a common occurrence. There should be no hard feelings, it is both a personal and a professional decision by Deaf people. In turn, interpreters maintain their professional demeanor and do not allow personal experience to interfere with their work; they stay neutral and interpret to the spirit of the message for all assignments.

Interpreters are required to maintain their membership with the RID. They must attend professional development workshops and conferences to maintain their certifications.

Respect for colleagues and consumers is equally important.

TIP

You can learn more about ASL interpreters and the RID by going to RID.org.

Chapter 15
Soliciting Social Justice

S ome people say that America is a melting pot, an assortment of goodies combined in one vessel all blending together. Other people say America is a salad bowl, a myriad of tasty morsels that are put together for an orchestra of good eats. If America is truly a salad bowl of various veggies, the ingredients may exist side by side, but some components may overshadow others. In life, this happens as well. We can coexist, but we may not be living to our full potential. The Deaf community has faced this very situation as they coexist with people who can hear (the hearing world). When the two groups come together, both American, they may share an American national culture, but there have been conflicts. After all, ASL is another language that's independent from English, and the Deaf rely upon it for survival. But the majority of Americans use English, and the needs of those who use ASL are often overlooked.

This chapter explains with some detail what the Deaf community has faced at a global level, a historical level, and a scholastic level. The rest of the story is what they are doing about it as Americans. Social justice has never met a more determined people who love life, love their own language, and love living the American dream.

Oralists and Manualists Meet in Milan

In the early 1800s, many Deaf schools were established throughout the United States that still exist to this day. It was during this time that manual communication was prospering.

In 1880, a Conference for educators of the Deaf took place in Milan, Italy. This was a turning point for American Sign Language. At this meeting, about seven countries of educators for the Deaf were present, including the United States, Italy, Britain, and France, to name a few. This gathering is known as the Milan Conference or the Second International Congress. There were two schools of thought that dominated the Conference: Oralism and Manualism. Both of these philosophies had their own methods of teaching Deaf children, and each had their own supporters.

>> **Oralists** believed that lip reading, mouth movement/speech, and sound/auditory training were all needed to give Deaf people a complete education based on learning to speak first. This would impact how Deaf people communicate long after their primary education was complete. This method also dismissed Deaf culture, which is embedded in sign language. Oralists felt that manual communication, sign language, was a hindrance to language development. Alexander Graham Bell was one of the supporters of Oralist education.

>> **Manualists** believed that sign language, which has its own rules of grammar and structure and its own linguistic evolution, could fulfill all language requirements to teach Deaf children as it is a natural means to communicate.

A resolution at the Conference was passed that banned sign language from being used in schools to teach Deaf people. Many Deaf schools suffered from this decision and were closed. Deaf teachers were released, and non-signers were hired in their place.

France and Italy supported an Oralist method of teaching while Britain and the United States supported the Manualist method of teaching. Even though the Oralist won the battle of the day, the Manualist grew more resolute in their cause and solidarity.

American Sign Language has been preserved to this day in many schools for the Deaf in the U.S. and around the world.

The Deaf Have It

These days, many people are learning sign language. Although many people enjoy learning the beauty of the physical expression of ASL, the rich history of the language, and the unity of the Deaf community are braided together that make Deaf culture. We must remember that ASL is the language of the Deaf. In other words, it is theirs as orchestrators and guardians of ASL that we know today.

In Deaf history, the Deaf have fought long and hard against people who wish to ban sign language, view it as a marginal language, label it as a Tarzan language, or not give it language status at all. As language is tied to its native users, the Deaf are tied to ASL. This means that Deaf people are native users of ASL, and those who are not native users are linguistic guests in the world of this language. Therefore, it is to the benefit of all non-native ASL users to allow the Deaf to be their own experts of their language regardless of how long and deep a non-Deaf person has studied the ASL. Let the Deaf lead the way in the Deaf world. ASL has existed in the Unites States for almost 300 years, so it is a safe assumption that the Deaf community knows what they are doing.

REMEMBER

Those who are not native ASL users must be polite linguistic guests. Like any guest, is your host happy that you are coming to visit or happy that you are leaving?

Rejecting Language Oppression

Oppression occurs when someone dominates another. The dominating person takes away the oppressed person's ability to make choices or share in the decision making. Although oppression is often seen in ethnic groups, it is also seen with people who can hear, the hearing, and people who cannot hear, the Deaf. Since culturally Deaf people, those who rely on ASL to communicate, view themselves as an ethnic group with their own history, language, and culture, oppression against them can be viewed as an ethnic oppression. Specifically, since the hearing people have dominated ASL by taking away Deaf people's choices about ASL, this action can be viewed as language oppression.

Oppression has occurred when hearing people do not include Deaf people in deciding how they should be educated (as in the Milan Conference mentioned earlier in this chapter.) Oppression also takes the form of not viewing ASL as an independent and equal language to verbal languages and not understanding that ASL is a bona fide language with its own culture and evolutionary process.

Here is another example of the oppression of Deaf people and their language: In 1988, Gallaudet University — the only Deaf liberal arts university in the world — selected a new President for the seventh time in its history. This person was not

Deaf but could hear and was not a representation of the Deaf student population. In an outrage, students, faculty, and alumni, protested until their cries were heard. The protestors shut the school down until their demands were met. This movement was known as Deaf President Now (DPN). To meet the student population's demands, Dr. I. King Jordan was named the new and the eighth President of Gallaudet University, and he is Deaf.

How can you reject language oppression?

>> Develop an awareness of how Deaf people have been oppressed.

>> Remember that ASL is an equal language, and the Deaf are the experts of ASL.

Movers and Shakers

The world of entertainment has never been more diverse and vibrant. Deaf people are riding this train as it stops in everyone's homes when we turn on the television or computer and watch our favorite dancers, actors, athletes, and, cooks. Language is not the only contribution that Deaf people give our American community; Deaf people are going to studios and stadiums with their talents.

From reality television to world arenas, the Deaf community is participating in full force. Examples of Deaf people breaking the barrier into mainstream entertainment include

>> Heather Whitestone McCallum, Miss America 1995

>> Kenny Walker, defensive lineman, Denver Broncos

>> Kurt "Irish Chef" Ramborger, Food Network's "Chopped"

>> Nyle DiMarco of "Dancing with the Stars"

>> Matt "The Hammer" Hamill, UFC Champion.

These talented people have opened doors and have given other Deaf people examples to live up to. They lead the way for others who wish to aspire beyond their own community. Their work also brings people from the hearing world into the Deaf world. These encounters allow non-signers to meet Deaf people out of their community element where they exchange ideas, get to know each other, and find that Deaf people have families, bills, political perspectives, and fears. That's where people learn about how to relate to one another, and social injustice ceases to exist when we come together and understand that we share a common humanity and deserve equal treatment.

Chapter 16

Using Technology to Communicate

Times are changing. Technology has changed society, and the Deaf community is not far behind. At one time, Deaf people depended on the hearing world to help them place phone calls when the need arose. They had to use an interpreter, who stood in front of them and interpreted any and all information that the Deaf person required. Later on, the Deaf community could use a teletype machine, or TTY, to communicate information through an operator who had good typing skills but knew nothing of deafness, American Sign Language, or the role of an interpreter. However, through the advancement of technology, Deaf people now have several more options for communicating with friends, family, and business contacts — hearing or deaf — whether they're at home or out and about.

In this chapter, I acquaint you with the latest communication devices that have not only brought Deaf people independence but also opened a door that can never be closed again.

Using Videophones: Can You See Me Now?

The videophone has replaced the TTY for Deaf people calling friends and family, making appointments, and attending to daily business needs. To set up a videophone, all you need is a videophone, internet connection, and a screen to connect the VP, or videophone. Deaf people do have the option, however, of having an application on their smartphones. A simple click of a button and one can download a means to chat with others via their phones. Video phones, the ones that are left at home, are given without cost from some communication companies.

TIP

Videophones allow a Deaf person to call another Deaf person without the use of an interpreter. If a Deaf person is calling a person who can hear, an ASL interpreter will answer the phone and process the call. With that, do not be alarmed if a man is calling with a woman's voice, it is just the interpreter.

Videophone technology changes rapidly, so it's best to read up on videophones on the Internet to see what kind of phone and service would best fit your needs. In many cases, a videophone is free for Deaf people. Start your search by typing in "videophones" on the Internet. You will see the information and options available.

Several companies provide videophones. These companies have their own equipment, technicians, and procedures for how they govern their operations. Any agency that operates a video relay service (VRS) must follow the Federal Communications Commission (FCC) guidelines for how it conducts its business.

Communicating with videophones

Deaf people can communicate using the videophone in one of two ways:

>> **Communicating directly:** If two people have videophones, they can communicate directly with each other. Many Deaf people have videophones, so if Deaf friends want to talk to each other, they can just call without having to use any kind of relay service.

The system can have glitches — the camera may freeze, a disconnection may occur, or the picture may not be as clear as it should be. These problems may be common, but they also happen when hearing people communicate with each other on any phone system or on a video device as well.

>> **Communicating via a relay interpreter:** If a hearing person doesn't have a videophone but wants to talk to a Deaf person, the two of them need an interpreter who has a compatible device.

These relay interpreters work for one of several companies that provide telecommunication services. To work for one of these businesses, interpreters need to show that they have satisfied the minimum requirements of ASL competency. This requires being able to understand what a Deaf person is signing and to sign to the Deaf person what the hearing person is saying.

If two Deaf people want to converse but only one has a videophone, it's not uncommon for the person without the videophone to use one at the local library, a friend's home, or any agency that has a videophone. In short, two people must both have videophones to make contact to visually communicate.

However, a Deaf person can also use a TTY to call a videophone (for more on the TTY, see the nearby sidebar). The TTY caller dials the operator through a designated phone number, and the TTY operator calls the video relay service. The relay interpreter then contacts the Deaf person who has the videophone. This is a four way conversation: the Deaf person using the TTY, the TTY operator, the relay interpreter, and the Deaf caller on the videophone.

What to expect when using a video relay service

Using a video relay service is a straightforward process. A person calls the VRS, and the interpreter connects the call. When the other person answers, the interpreter begins the interpreting process.

Keep in mind that this is a video relay, and the Deaf person and the interpreter can see each other. Because the process involves two modes of language — one verbal and one visual — there's a slight time delay to go from one language to the other.

REMEMBER

The interpreter will speak as though she's the person on the other end of the line, so although it may feel strange at first, respond to the interpreter that way. Don't ask the interpreter to tell your friend something; just tell your friend, and the interpreter will take care of signing it for you. In a nutshell, act like the interpreter isn't there and talk directly to your party.

Don't get confused. The terms *operator* and *interpreter* are often used interchange-ably on video relay; the relay interpreter/operator knows ASL, but a TTY operator is an operator who doesn't sign.

Keeping quiet what is private

A VRS interpreter who is certified by the Registry of Interpreters for the Deaf (RID) must abide by the Code of Professional Conduct. The most important part of the RID Code is the need to keep information confidential. This is a trust issue, and all interpreters doing any type of interpreting work must follow the Code. So an interpreter cannot repeat information obtained during an assignment (each vid-eophone call is considered an assignment).

If an interpreter violates this trust, the violation may be reported to the RID in the form of a grievance. The RID takes this type of complaint very seriously.

Using Other Communication Methods

Today, Deaf people can communicate with other Deaf people (and with hearing people as well) in numerous ways. With Skype, Fring, and other mobile applica-tions, Deaf people are no longer tied to primarily using a homebound telephone.

Texting 24/7

Today, many Deaf people use texting for everyday communication. Mobile phones are small and compact, which makes them easy to carry. Deaf people can text throughout the day to anyone who has the same capability. With this technology, Deaf people can send not only text messages but also photos and video clips.

A word to the wise: even though you erase your text messages, there is always a record somewhere.

Telecommunication businesses that sell phones and phone services have the capability to offer communication applications that allow Deaf people and hearing people to use video to communicate. Ask your phone company about this capabil-ity or just look through your phone applications.

WEBCAMS FOR DESKTOPS

Many laptops and tablets, and pretty much every modern smartphone, have built-in cameras that enable the device to act as videophone on the go provided you have a fast internet connection. Desktop computers provide a more powerful, yet stationary, option for computing. Since many desktops often don't have a built-in camera, you can buy an external webcam to add videophone capabilities. Most webcams are compatible with Skype, but check with the manufacturer before you buy.

Chatting visually

Deaf people often communicate through text, e-mails, or even a fax, but these are still English-based modes and not the primary language of Deaf people. Deaf people welcome communication devices that are visually based and allow them the opportunity to communicate in ASL.

Skype is a popular method of chatting for personal and professional matters. This software program allows users to see each other to communicate anywhere in the world. Communication can take place in spoken English or in Sign. With an internet connection and a computer, tablet, or smartphone, you can access Skype and chat with anyone who also has the software. Deaf people can use Skype like a videophone without an interpreter.

Calling through Captioning

Making phone calls as a Deaf person is an interesting event. Some Deaf people use a videophone to see who they are conversing with while other Deaf people would rather talk to other people using a traditional telephone. The question is, how do Deaf people use a house phone/landline if they cannot hear?

Deafness comes at different levels. While some Deaf people have less residual hearing than other Deaf people, still others can hear clearer than others and may speak for themselves without an interpreter. Nonetheless, there are phone devices that allow Deaf people to read what is being said by the other party and verbally enjoy phone conversation. What's more, if you have a smartphone, you can download an app to receive phone captioning. Or you can purchase a home phone with call captioning or even enable this feature on your personal computer. Call captioning allows a person to read what is being said. The subtitled conversation appears across the phone screen, enabling anyone to have uninterrupted conversation. Some phone devices will allow the caller to increase sound volume, store phone numbers, show previous calls, show who is calling, and speakerphone options to allow the caller to make lunch and still be engaged in chitchat.

For call captioning, there are two avenues: 1-line mode and 2-line mode. Either way, it is a simple process. If a person calling does not have captioning capability, they call an 800 phone number to reach a call center, and then they enter the phone number of whom they are calling. The call is connected and captioning may begin. The captioning is typed by a specially trained person. If both parties have captioning capability, this is a 2-line mode and a caller does not need to call a call center for captioning service.

There are many companies that act as providers for captioned calls. Make sure that whichever company you choose is registered with the FCC, which means they follow standards of practice that ensure quality service and privacy.

4

The Part of Tens

Chapter 17

Ten Tips to Help You Sign like a Pro

This chapter is all about providing you with ideas to practice and polish your signing skills. So if you're reading this, you're on the right track.

Watch Yourself and Others Sign

Recording yourself sign helps you see what others see when you sign. Watching interpreters lets you see how they make facial expressions and how they use signs in context. Watching others sign also gives you the opportunity to *read* how they sign. Standing in front of a mirror is helpful, but it is real time and you can't go back and see the terrific job you did or where you would like to improve. However, recording yourself allows that opportunity. Keep in mind, you can be your own worst critic or your biggest fan; it is all in the perspective.

Discover Multiple Signs for Communicating One Thing

You can sign one thing in many different ways. The more ways you know, the more versatile you'll be. Even if a particular sign doesn't suit you, someone else may use it, so it's helpful to know it. For example, you can sign **do** in a number of ways. Ask a person who's been signing for a few years to show them to you. Keep a mental file of various signs that you observe, and soon you will possess a wealth of information that will allow you to be a resource for other signers.

Practice Your Signing — with Others

There's no substitute for practice. Use your time wisely by taking every opportunity to ask questions and fingerspell every advertisement sign. And go out of your way to meet as many Deaf people as possible. Sure, having a formal education in American Sign Language makes you a better signer, but practicing your skills with the Deaf person on the street can teach you things that a formal education can't, such as Deaf culture and Deaf idioms in action. Set yourself up for success: When you are fingerspelling, start with small simple words and graduate to longer ones. When you are fluid with the smaller ones, you will see the improvement.

Always Fingerspell a Name First

CULTURAL WISDOM

Name signs serve as identification and were originally used to talk about someone when the person wasn't present. The Deaf community — not hearing folks — gives name signs, which may be based on a person's initials, physical characteristics, or personality traits. However, a person's name must be established before you can use his name sign or talk about him. If you don't fingerspell a person's name first, you'll only cause confusion as to whom you mean.

Adjust Your Eyes; Everyone's Signing Is Different

Personalities tend to come out in Sign, just as they do in English. Some people talk fast and sign fast, and others want to give you all the details. Just as no two people talk alike, no two signers sign alike. By being open to the different ways that people sign, you can grow to understand the variety of signing styles as easily as you can understand most English speakers in the United States. If you don't understand someone at first, don't give up; get the context of what they are talking about, adjust your eyes to their signing, and be patient. Skill is its own reward.

Use Facial Expressions like Vocal Inflections

Imagine talking without any high or low pitches — speaking only in a monotone, with few clues to emphasize your point. Your conversation would be boring and hard to understand. The same holds true when you sign. If you sign about someone being angry, look angry!

If you want to convey your joy, you need to show that joy, and if something scary happened to you, look scared! As a general rule, the clearest facial expression is an authentic one. You achieve this by practicing actual expressions: Put on a big smile for joy, frown when you want to show sadness or unhappiness, and frown and scrunch your eyebrows together to convey a feeling of anger.

REMEMBER

If you are not an emotional person by nature, flip through magazine advertisements and see all the different expressions people use for different circumstances. These are paid actors, they know how to work it.

Journal Your Progress

Keeping track of your linguistic experiences — the good and the bad, the conflicts and resolutions — helps you map your progress and remember the ins and outs of Deaf culture. In your journal, maintain a separate section of terms and the various ways of signing different concepts; that helps you compare the similarities and differences among terms and concepts, expand your vocabulary, and see the bigger picture of the Deaf world. Sharing your journal with a certain Deaf person whose signing abilities you aspire to imitate is a great compliment to the person. But make sure you change the names in the conflicts and resolutions part to protect the innocent!

Get Some Signing Space

Signing and talking affect where you sit or stand. Because signing is manual, give signers a little room to converse. If you need privacy, go somewhere private to have your conversation. And make sure that you don't stand with bright light or the sun directly behind you, because whoever is watching you sign will only see your silhouette — a big giveaway that you're just a beginner.

CULTURAL WISDOM

Because ASL is a physical language, two signers having a conversation need more space than hearing people do. Also, walking right between two people who are signing is perfectly acceptable in the Deaf world; you don't need to say "excuse me."

Don't Jump the Gun

Sometimes, when you're watching someone sign, you may lose that person and not understand her meaning. Don't lose heart. Try to let the person finish the thought; you may put it all together at the very end, after she has finished signing all the information. Then, if you still don't understand, just explain that you didn't catch everything, and let the person know what you did catch. (*Note:* Stopping someone and asking for clarification or waiting until the person is finished to see if you can make sense of things are two techniques used by many signers and interpreters. Both techniques have a place in Sign.)

So breathe, stay calm, and ask specific questions for clarity. This is how you develop your confidence.

Watch the Face, Not the Hands

You can find most of what you need to know on a signer's face. A person's face conveys moods, pauses, any information that can be demonstrated through mouth shapes, and how an action is done (slowly, quickly, sloppily, and so on). If you focus on a signer's hands, you miss a lot of crucial information; instead, focus on the signer's face and shoulders. Use your peripheral vision to watch the hands. By doing this, you see the whole signer, and you're apt to better understand the conversation. On an added note, signers can point with their eyes so watch the complete person.

Chapter 18

Ten Ways to Pick Up Sign Quickly

S igning with your friends has never been easier. You have natural signs and gestures to make your point. You also have this book to add to what you already know. This chapter is short, but it gives you great ideas for some of the things you can do if you want to pick up American Sign Language a little more quickly.

Volunteer at a Residential School for the Deaf

One way to immerse yourself in the Deaf world is to volunteer at a residential school for the Deaf. Deaf culture is the way of life at these schools, and by being exposed to the culture, you become intimately familiar with Sign. You can volunteer for after-school recreation programs or special-event preparations. Schools can never have too many volunteers to act as scorekeepers, coaches, assistants, ticket sellers, and other positions. By interacting with Deaf students, teachers, and parents, you'll measurably improve both your expressive (signing to others) and receptive (reading others' signs) signing.

REMEMBER

Know that Deaf residential schools are a culture within the Deaf culture. There are name signs known to people who work there and every day name signs for happenings in their daily lives, this information is known to them. If you are there but a couple of days a week, it will be added information to learn. However, to immerse into the Deaf world and Deaf culture, a residential school is a perfect place to volunteer. Be patient with yourself and be open to learning; they would love to have you.

Volunteer at Local Deaf Clubs

Many Deaf people tend to congregate at their own clubs for a variety of reasons. They socialize, play pool, go on trips, and watch TV, just to name a few activities. Many Deaf people bring their hearing children to these clubs so they can practice their signing and learn the ways of the Deaf culture. Some clubs even have photo albums of past members and guests. Deaf clubs also have fundraising events fairly often. Volunteering at one of these fundraisers is a great opportunity to practice signing while helping others. Volunteers are always needed to sell raffle tickets, take tickets during an event, keep score at games, or simply serve refreshments.

Attend Deaf Social Functions

Social functions are becoming more common since more Deaf people have started specialized organizations. These events vary from sports activities to Deaf camp-outs to raffles. People interested in helping with flyers and tickets are always welcome. You can find out about functions in your community by checking the community pages in the phone book, searching the Internet, or calling the local residential school for the Deaf, if your community has one.

Although it is appropriate to be invited by a Deaf person first, social functions are a great place to make friends. Mix and mingle, let people know who invited you and that you're interested in ASL. For the beginner, common topics can be Gallaudet University, ASL, the local Deaf club, and Deaf people who are on reality shows. Don't be surprised if some Deaf people at these functions know Deaf television personalities, it is a small, tight community.

TIP

It's customary to have a Deaf friend accompany you to one of these events, so that he or she can introduce you to Deaf people for the first time. Take advantage of this and branch out, soon enough these very people will be inviting you.

Make Deaf Friends

Having Deaf friends is really no different from having hearing friends. Many Deaf people enjoy watching and playing sports, going shopping, and surfing the Internet. A Deaf friend can help you a lot with ASL. Just think carefully about your friendship, though. Deaf people are sharing a language and culture with you that they hold in high regard; please try to do the same.

Assist Deaf Ministries

Attending Deaf churches and Deaf ministries is a sure way to meet Deaf people. Watching religious interpreters in these settings keeps you on the cutting edge of Sign vocabulary. Some churches that have large Deaf ministries have programs set up for members of their congregation who want to interpret for the Deaf. Church activities, such as picnics and Deaf Bible study groups, are enjoyable activities where you can offer your assistance or simply watch the preaching in Sign. Helping the interpreters is always a kind gesture, often getting water for the working interpreters, helping them look up key words as they prepare for the sermon, and greeting the Deaf as they arrive will be a sure way to show you care. Watch the interpreters as they work, take notes, they may even mentor you!

Attend Conferences for Interpreters

Sign language interpreting conferences are held every year in each state. These conferences feature workshops and breakout sessions on various topics, incorporating the latest research on interpreting, ASL, and more. The conferences also usually have evening entertainment performances by Deaf people and hearing people alike. Attending one of these conferences is an excellent way to pick up information about interpreting, sharpen your ASL skills, and meet other people who are learning Sign. You'll also find booths with work opportunities, silent auctions, and mentoring opportunities by professional interpreters.

Work at Camps for the Deaf

Working at a Deaf camp gives the novice signer a relaxed atmosphere in which to work with Deaf children. Deaf camps are filled with fun activities such as games and hiking. You have ample opportunity to interact with Deaf people from different areas and to encounter a variety of signing styles and jargon. You may even get the opportunity to see both adults and children perform stories in Sign. Who knows, during a week of camp you may even form new friendships that last long after camp has ended.

Attend Silent Weekends

Silent weekends aren't as lengthy as Deaf camps. Beginning signers who can't miss time from work may find these weekends a perfect opportunity to mix with the Deaf community. These weekends vary as to how they're run. Some furnish cabins that allow people to talk in the evenings, usually after 4 or 6 p.m., while others allow no talking at all. In fact, you may even be fined — 10 or 25 cents per infraction — if you're caught talking! Entertainment is on hand, and an array of ASL teachers and interpreters are available to ensure that the weekend is filled with accurate signing. There are local and national speakers who attend these events, and audience participants come from all over the country. This is a good way to see a variety of signs, watch talented speakers who are well versed in ASL, and practice what you are learning.

TIP

You can obtain information about these silent weekends by going to the Internet and look for your state's interpreter association. Each state has a chapter of the Registry of Interpreters for the Deaf (RID). Click your state's link for information.

Go to Deaf Workshops and Deaf Conferences

Many Deaf organizations exist, and one in particular is the National Association of the Deaf (NAD). Workshops and conferences take place through these organizations and offer a myriad of subjects — something to interest everyone. One popular subject is Sign itself. Many educators and veteran interpreters regularly present poetry in Sign or give in-depth analyses of particular properties of Sign. Attending one of these workshops may give you new insights into Deaf culture.

Like Silent Weekends, conferences and workshops are a great place to practice your signing, although you are allowed to speak at these events. You will find much socializing at these events and many gifted presenters will be present. Some may use interpreters who voice what they are signing. Take advantage of this!

Watch the presenters and listen to the interpreters. You will understand more clearly how professional interpreters read Deaf signers and how they process information. Do not be discouraged if you cannot keep up with their skill. They are voicing for the Deaf speakers because they are professionally trained so take what you can and pat yourself on the back for doing your best. Trying is a requirement to success.

Watch Sign Language Videos

Videos are a sure way to improve your signing. Many companies specialize in ASL materials and are happy to send you their catalogs. Get together with a Deaf friend, grab a catalog, and let your friend help you decide which videos would be good to learn from based on your particular level of ability. The best way to find sources of these types of videos is to surf the Internet. Just enter the words "sign language" into your search engine and watch how many sites come up. Your local library is also a good source for videos. Although books are a big help, videos have the capacity to demonstrate three-dimensional signing, and you can also rewind them and view them in slow motion for easier learning. Besides, viewing one of these videos with a friend can be a lot of fun.

Chapter 19

Ten Popular Deaf Expressions

American Sign Language uses expressions in much the same way that English does. However, in ASL expressions are stated manually, which means that they are seen differently. This chapter describes some expressions that are commonly used in Sign. Practicing these expressions with people who've been signing for a while can be a shortcut to your success.

Some of the following signs have an exact English equivalent and some don't. The ones that don't, however, are quite similar to an English expression. Watch how Deaf people use these expressions in context. In ASL there are many ways to share an expression, here are only a handful.

REMEMBER

Swallowed the Fish

This idiom indicates gullibility. You use it in good humor after someone mistakenly places his trust in someone he shouldn't have or should have known something since it is common knowledge. You can sign it about yourself or about another person. When you sign it, widen your eyes as if to show embarrassment due to the gullibility.

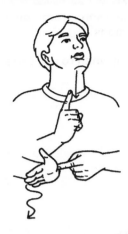

Train Gone

You don't normally direct this lighthearted idiom toward yourself but rather toward someone else. You often use this sign, which can be compared to the English idiom "missed the boat," when someone tells a joke and everyone laughs except one person, or when one person wants something repeated that everyone else understood the first time. In these moments, someone will look at the person who doesn't get it, smile, and sign **train gone**. The facial expression for this sign can be puffed cheeks (imitating a smokestack) or just a blank stare, whichever you prefer. Either way, everyone will know that someone didn't catch the information.

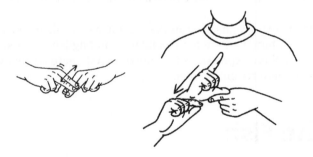

Pea Brain

Hearing people use this idiom as well, and just as in English, you shouldn't use this idiom very often because it's not polite. In fact, it's somewhat offensive, although perhaps in a group of good friends you can get away with it if you mean it in good fun. The facial expression that accompanies this sign determines the degree of meaning or, in this case, maybe the size of one's brain! Sticking out your flattened tongue while signing **pea brain** makes your meaning pretty clear. What's even meaner is crossing your eyes while showing the sign. So as a general rule, save this sign for people you know really well. You can also direct this sign at yourself in a self-deprecating manner when you do something stupid or state something that's obvious to everyone else.

Rats!/Darn!

If you've ever experienced a situation in which something doesn't go as expected, you probably already know how to use this expression. Like the illustration indicates, you open your passive hand facing up. Using your dominant hand, you start with the manual number 5 and, with the manual letter S, you act like you're catching a fly in the palm of your hand.

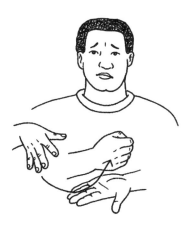

I Hope

To sign **I hope,** you cross your fingers on both hands. It's pretty simple and is generally understood in both the hearing and Deaf worlds alike. Just cross your fingers in R handshapes. You can add the facial expression of closing your eyes tightly and clenching your teeth or widening your eyes with your mouth slightly opened.

Your Guess Is as Good as Mine

This expression is used in English as well as Sign. In English, you use this expression only after someone asks a question. However, in Sign, you can ask a question and use this expression at the same time. A good facial expression to go with this sign is to smirk (smiling with just the corner of your mouth) and raise your eyebrows. Another way to emphasize this expression is to make the size of the sign bigger. Doing so tells whomever you're signing that you really don't have any idea whatsoever.

Cool!

This expression is also used in English as well as Sign. You can sign it in two different ways; both signs have pretty much the same meaning.

The first sign, shown in the following picture, is made by placing your index finger and thumb on your cheek and twisting your wrist in an inward motion. The facial expression can be a smile or pursed lips — as long as your attitude is positive, the facial expression will follow.

The second sign is made by putting your thumb on the center of your chest and wiggling the fingers, leaving your facial expression fully visible. Forming an "ooh" shape with your mouth means **really cool.** Opening your mouth wide can mean a **surprised cool.**

You will see Deaf people using both signs interchangeably.

Oh No!

Make this sign when you witness an embarrassing action or are explaining one of your own embarrassing actions to someone. Open your eyes wide; you can even put on a nervous smile as you express this sign. You make this sign with the manual 5 palm facing the signer and close it to make the manual S; it signifies a lump in your throat.

That's Superb!

This sign is made by using the manual −F handshape and touching the center of your chin. Your facial expression will tell if it is a positive experience or a negative one. Often the mouth makes an −OO shape to show your pleasure or that you are impressed. If you want to show that something is really bad, use this sign and have the facial expression as if to smell bad air. Your point will be quite clear.

That's Pretty Straight-Laced

By making this sign, you're saying that someone is ultraconservative, close-minded, or just an old-fashioned square. For your facial expression, press your lips tightly together, perhaps paired with a snobbish-type expression.

Wow!

You can use this expression with a positive or a negative connotation. Your facial expression, along with the conversation's context, tells your friends exactly how you feel about the subject at hand. Your eyes should be wide open, accompanied by a partial smile. You fingerspell W-O-W right next to the side of your open mouth. If your response is less than favorable, you crunch up your eyebrows.

Index

C

M

MANAGER (sign for), 39, 117, 222

MANAGERS MEETING (sign for), 232

manners, 47

manual handshape, 40, 131, 138, 142, 179, 214, 237, 271

Manualism, 298

MANY (sign for), 61

MARKETING – V-P (sign for), 121

MARRIED (sign for), 216

MATCH (sign for), 237, 238

MATINEE (sign for), 207

MAXIMUM (sign for), 200

MAYBE (sign for), 14

McCallum, Heather Whitestone (Miss America), 300

ME (sign for), 23

ME TOO (sign for), 52

mealtime, 150

MEAN (sign for), 105

MECHANIC (sign for), 119

medical field. See health

MEDICINE (sign for), 271

MEET ME (sign for), 122

MEETING/CONFERENCE (sign for), 225, 231

MEMORIAL DAY (sign for), 94

Mexican Sign Language, 164

MEXICO (sign for), 54

MIAMI (sign for), 56

MIDNIGHT (sign for), 206

Milan Conference, 298

MILK (sign for), 8, 167

MINE (sign for), 110

MINIMUM (sign for), 200

MINNESOTA (sign for), 56

mobile applications, 304

money, 194–196

MONEY (sign for), 195

MORNING (sign for), 72

MOTHER (sign for), 108

MOTHER'S DAY (sign for), 93

MOTORCYCLE (sign for), 142

MOTORCYCLE HELMET (sign for), 143

MOUNTAIN (sign for), 60, 61, 136

MOUTH (sign for), 273

mouth movement, 10, 45, 298

movers and shakers, 300

MOVIE/MOVIES (sign for), 106, 207

movies, going to, 206–211

MOVING YOU – WHERE Q (sign for), 114

MPH (sign for), 140

MUDSLIDE (sign for), 256

MUSEUM (sign for), 134, 213, 214

museum, going to, 213–215

MY, MINE (sign for), 123

MYSTERY (movie genre) (sign for), 208

N

name signs, 48, 310

NAPKIN (sign for), 148

National Association of the Deaf (NAD), 316

natural disasters, 255–256

natural handshapes, 12–13

natural landmarks, 135–138

natural signs, 8

NAUSEA (sign for), 266

NEAR (sign for), 132

NECK (sign for), 274

NEED US (sign for), 91

NEITHER (sign for), 146

neither/nor, 145

NEW YEAR'S (sign for), 94

NEW YORK (sign for), 56

NICE TO MEET YOU (sign for), 43, 48, 49, 121

NIGHT (sign for), 72

NINE (sign for), 68

NINETEEN (sign for), 68

NO (sign for), 15

NOON (sign for), 72, 206

NOON FOOD (sign for), 156, 157

NORTH (sign for), 130

TREE (sign for), 59, 136
TRUE (sign for), 42, 50
T-SHIRT (sign for), 179
TSUNAMI (sign for), 255
TTY (teletypes), 286, 301, 303, 304
TURN (sign for), 132
TWELVE (sign for), 68
TWILIGHT (sign for), 72
TWO (sign for), 67
TWO HOURS (sign for), 106
TWO MINUTES (sign for), 71
TWO O'CLOCK (sign for), 71

U

UMBRELLA (sign for), 183
UMPIRE (sign for), 237, 238
UNCLE (sign for), 109
UNCONSCIOUS (sign for), 266
underwear, 179
UNDERWEAR (sign for), 179
UNITED STATES/AMERICA (sign for), 54
UPSTAIRS (sign for), 81, 83, 232
urban landmarks, 139–141
US (sign for), 33, 124

V

VACATION (sign for), 96
VALENTINE'S DAY (sign for), 93
VASE (sign for), 88
verbs, 17, 18, 24, 42
VERSUS (sign for), 237
VICE PRESIDENT (sign for), 118, 119
video clips, 3, 10–11
VIDEO GAMES (sign for), 247
video relay service (VRS), 302, 303
videophone (VP), 301–304
videos, 317
volunteering (to sign), 314

W

WAITER/WAITRESS/SERVER (sign for), 119, 163
Walker, Kenny (NFL player), 300
WALKING (sign for), 243
WALLET (sign for), 183
WARNING (sign for), 256
was, as not used in ASL, 42
WATER (sign for), 158, 167
WATERFALL (sign for), 137
WE, US (sign for), 124
WEAR (sign for), 176
WEATHER (sign for), 255
weather reports, 254–255, 257–258
webcams, 305
were, as not used in ASL, 42
WEST (sign for), 130
WHAT (sign for), 32
WHAT? (sign for), 103
WHAT'S UP (sign for), 45
WHEELCHAIR (sign for), 271
WHEN? (sign for), 103
when, idea of, 70
WHERE? (sign for), 103
where you're from, talking about, 53–61
WHICH? (sign for), 104
WHISKEY/ALCOHOL (sign for), 167
WHITE (sign for), 89, 178, 189
WHO? (sign for), 103
WHY? (sign for), 104
WIDOW/WIDOWER (sign for), 217
WILL (sign for), 30
WINDOW (sign for), 80, 82
WINDY (sign for), 255
WINE (sign for), 36–37, 167
WIN/WON (sign for), 239
WISDOM/WISE (sign for), 127
WORK (sign for), 231
work colleagues, 111

About the Authors

Adan R. Penilla II, PhD, NAD IV, CI/CT, NIC, and SC:L, is currently employed as an ASL video relay interpreter. He is an adjunct professor of ASL at Colorado State University. He also works in the Colorado legal system as an interpreter.

Dr. Penilla was an interpreter at the World Federation of the Deaf in Vienna (1995). His publications include *ASL Quick Study Barcharts, The Middle East in ASL, Countries from around the World in ASL,* and *Cities from around the World in ASL.*

Some lectures he has authored include "Prosody and Placement of Gestures in American Sign Language and English," "Name Sign Properties in ASL," "Invisible Boundaries of Mental Health interpreting," "Turmoil over Eastern Europe," and "Out of Africa and into the Hot Seat in ASL."

He was a presenter at the National RID Conferences in Atlanta (2011) and Indianapolis (2013). He has presented at the National Silent weekend in Florida in 2014, 2015, and, 2016.

He presents throughout the United States to interpreters of ASL.

Angela Lee Taylor, born deaf, is a native of Dixon, Illinois. Taylor graduated from the Illinois School for the Deaf in 1985 and received her bachelor's degree from Gallaudet University in 1997. Taylor has taught ASL for Pikes Peak Community College, the Colorado School for the Deaf and the Blind, and the community.

Author's Acknowledgments

To my family of many directions, we come together to celebrate life and its rich encounters. How blessed I am to know each of you. My five adorable sisters, you compete amongst one another at every turn and close ranks when anyone comes to comment. I admire your bond. Thank you for your support.

Dad, your friendship is constantly making me think two steps ahead. I needed that for the completion of this book. Thank you.

Mom, although you are not here anymore, a day does not go by when I don't think of you. Your constant demand that I do my best and give my all is the reason why I agreed to write this book. I find myself digging deeper and pushing further to honor your memory when I need that extra strength. I miss you.

Lindsay Lefevere and Tim Gallan, my editors, thank you for the advice, patience, and constant explanation as this book came together. Although this is my third book, your talent and feedback are what was needed most. Thanks for being a great team. Without your help, none of this would have happened.

Leland Paul Reeck, ID, your dedication, constant advice and ever tracking radar in all my endeavors are what brought this book together. Your knowledge, talent, and wisdom have called me to heights that I only imagined. It is an honor to be your friend and confidant for so many years. Thanks for everything.

— Adan R. Penilla

Dedication

To the American military and all the families who support our troops, I dedicate this book. You keep us safe from the dark shadow of uncertainty that is plaguing the world. We tend to not think of our freedom, and that's a testament to how well you do your jobs. Democracy has no better allies than those who guard it.

Publisher's Acknowledgments

Executive Editor: Lindsay Lefevere

Project Editor: Tim Gallan

Technical Reviewer: Leland Paul Reeck

Illustrator: Lisa Reed

Art Coordinator: Alicia B. South

Production Editor: Kumar Chellappan

Cover Image: © RapidEye/Getty Images, Inc.

Apple & Mac

iPad For Dummies,
6th Edition
978-1-118-72306-7

iPhone For Dummies,
7th Edition
978-1-118-69083-3

Macs All-in-One
For Dummies, 4th Edition
978-1-118-82210-4

OS X Mavericks
For Dummies
978-1-118-69188-5

Blogging & Social Media

Facebook For Dummies,
5th Edition
978-1-118-63312-0

Social Media Engagement
For Dummies
978-1-118-53019-1

WordPress For Dummies,
6th Edition
978-1-118-79161-5

Business

Stock Investing
For Dummies, 4th Edition
978-1-118-37678-2

Investing For Dummies,
6th Edition
978-0-470-90545-6

Personal Finance
For Dummies, 7th Edition
978-1-118-11785-9

QuickBooks 2014
For Dummies
978-1-118-72005-9

Small Business Marketing
Kit For Dummies,
3rd Edition
978-1-118-31183-7

Careers

Job Interviews
For Dummies, 4th Edition
978-1-118-11290-8

Job Searching with Social
Media For Dummies,
2nd Edition
978-1-118-67856-5

Personal Branding
For Dummies
978-1-118-11792-7

Resumes For Dummies,
6th Edition
978-0-470-87361-8

Starting an Etsy Business
For Dummies, 2nd Edition
978-1-118-59024-9

Diet & Nutrition

Belly Fat Diet For Dummies
978-1-118-34585-6

Mediterranean Diet
For Dummies
978-1-118-71525-3

Nutrition For Dummies,
5th Edition
978-0-470-93231-5

Digital Photography

Digital SLR Photography
All-in-One For Dummies,
2nd Edition
978-1-118-59082-9

Digital SLR Video &
Filmmaking For Dummies
978-1-118-36598-4

Photoshop Elements 12
For Dummies
978-1-118-72714-0

Gardening

Herb Gardening
For Dummies, 2nd Edition
978-0-470-61778-6

Gardening with Free-Range
Chickens For Dummies
978-1-118-54754-0

Health

Boosting Your Immunity
For Dummies
978-1-118-40200-9

Diabetes For Dummies,
4th Edition
978-1-118-29447-5

Living Paleo For Dummies
978-1-118-29405-5

Big Data

Big Data For Dummies
978-1-118-50422-2

Data Visualization
For Dummies
978-1-118-50289-1

Hadoop For Dummies
978-1-118-60755-8

Language &
Foreign Language

500 Spanish Verbs
For Dummies
978-1-118-02382-2

English Grammar
For Dummies, 2nd Edition
978-0-470-54664-2

French All-in-One
For Dummies
978-1-118-22815-9

German Essentials
For Dummies
978-1-118-18422-6

Italian For Dummies,
2nd Edition
978-1-118-00465-4

 **Available in print and e-book formats.**

Math & Science

Algebra I For Dummies,
2nd Edition
978-0-470-55964-2

Anatomy and Physiology
For Dummies, 2nd Edition
978-0-470-92326-9

Astronomy For Dummies,
3rd Edition
978-1-118-37697-3

Biology For Dummies,
2nd Edition
978-0-470-59875-7

Chemistry For Dummies,
2nd Edition
978-1-118-00730-3

1001 Algebra II Practice
Problems For Dummies
978-1-118-44662-1

Microsoft Office

Excel 2013 For Dummies
978-1-118-51012-4

Office 2013 All-in-One
For Dummies
978-1-118-51636-2

PowerPoint 2013
For Dummies
978-1-118-50253-2

Word 2013 For Dummies
978-1-118-49123-2

Music

Blues Harmonica
For Dummies
978-1-118-25269-7

Guitar For Dummies,
3rd Edition
978-1-118-11554-1

iPod & iTunes
For Dummies, 10th Edition
978-1-118-50864-0

Programming

Beginning Programming
with C For Dummies
978-1-118-73763-7

Excel VBA Programming
For Dummies, 3rd Edition
978-1-118-49037-2

Java For Dummies,
6th Edition
978-1-118-40780-6

Religion & Inspiration

The Bible For Dummies
978-0-7645-5296-0

Buddhism For Dummies,
2nd Edition
978-1-118-02379-2

Catholicism For Dummies,
2nd Edition
978-1-118-07778-8

Self-Help &
Relationships

Beating Sugar Addiction
For Dummies
978-1-118-54645-1

Meditation For Dummies,
3rd Edition
978-1-118-29144-3

Seniors

Laptops For Seniors
For Dummies, 3rd Edition
978-1-118-71105-7

Computers For Seniors
For Dummies, 3rd Edition
978-1-118-11553-4

iPad For Seniors
For Dummies, 6th Edition
978-1-118-72826-0

Social Security
For Dummies
978-1-118-20573-0

Smartphones & Tablets

Android Phones
For Dummies, 2nd Edition
978-1-118-72030-1

Nexus Tablets
For Dummies
978-1-118-77243-0

Samsung Galaxy S 4
For Dummies
978-1-118-64222-1

Samsung Galaxy Tabs
For Dummies
978-1-118-77294-2

Test Prep

ACT For Dummies,
5th Edition
978-1-118-01259-8

ASVAB For Dummies,
3rd Edition
978-0-470-63760-9

GRE For Dummies,
7th Edition
978-0-470-88921-3

Officer Candidate Tests
For Dummies
978-0-470-59876-4

Physician's Assistant Exam
For Dummies
978-1-118-11556-5

Series 7 Exam For Dummies
978-0-470-09932-2

Windows 8

Windows 8.1 All-in-One
For Dummies
978-1-118-82087-2

Windows 8.1 For Dummies
978-1-118-82121-3

Windows 8.1 For Dummies,
Book + DVD Bundle
978-1-118-82107-7

Available in print and e-book formats.

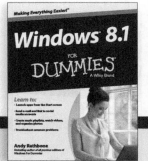

Available wherever books are sold. **For more information or to order direct visit www.dummies.com**

Take Dummies with you everywhere you go!

Whether you are excited about e-books, want more from the web, must have your mobile apps, or are swept up in social media, Dummies makes everything easier.

For Dummies is the global leader in the reference category and one of the most trusted and highly regarded brands in the world. No longer just focused on books, customers now have access to the For Dummies content they need in the format they want. Let us help you develop a solution that will fit your brand and help you connect with your customers.

Advertising & Sponsorships

Connect with an engaged audience on a powerful multimedia site, and position your message alongside expert how-to content.

Targeted ads • Video • Email marketing • Microsites • Sweepstakes sponsorship

Printed and bound by CPI Group (UK) Ltd, Croydon, CR0 4YY

09/06/2025

14685923-0003